INTERNATIONAL HARVESTER

TRACTOR

DATA BOOK

Guy Fay

MOTORBOOKS
INTERNATIONAL

This edition first published in 1997 by Motorbooks International,
an imprint of MBI Publishing Company, Galtier Plaza, Suite 200,
380 Jackson Street, St. Paul, MN 55101-3885 USA

The information in this book is true and complete to the best of our
knowledge. All recommendations are made without any guarantee on the
part of the author or Publisher, who also disclaim any liability incurred in
connection with the use of this data or specific details.

We recognize that some words, model names and designations, for
example, mentioned herein are the property of the trademark holder. We
use them for identification purposes only. This is not an official
publication.

Motorbooks International titles are also available at discounts in bulk
quantity for industrial or sales-promotional use. For details write to Special
Sales Manager at Motorbooks International Wholesalers & Distributors,
Galtier Plaza, Suite 200, 380 Jackson Street, St. Paul, MN 55101-3885
USA.

Library of Congress Cataloging-in-Publication Data

Fay, Guy.
     International-Harvester tractor data book/ Guy Fay.
          p. cm.
     Includes index.
     ISBN 0-7603-0321-5 (pbk. : alk. paper)
     1. IHC tractors—Specifications. 2. IHC tractors—History.
     I. Title
     TL233.6.I38F377   1997
     629.225'2--dc21   97-40001

On the front cover: The venerable Farmall H on the cover is at work on
International Harvester's experimental farm near Hinsdale, Illinois. *State
Historical Society of Wisconsin*

On the back cover: This I-4 is pulling a compacter along a new roadway.
The I-4, like all industrial tractors, lived a rough life. This one looks as if its
grille was just recently replaced. *State Historical Society of Wisconsin*

Printed in the United States of America

Contents

Acknowledgments

As with any book, thanks goes out to many, many people: the folks at Motorbooks (my long-suffering editor, Lee Klancher, among others), the people at the State Historical Society of Wisconsin (Cindy Knight, the IH Archivist, of course, but also the people who helped process the photo order, including Nicolette Bromberg, Andy Kraushaar, Scott Portman, and Nez Zaragoitia), the folks at Case IH (Dave Rodgers, Steve Hile, and Rich Saraga), and the folks who did fact checking at various stages—Ken Updike, Jim Becker, Scott Saterlund, and LeRoy Baumgardner (although, of course, all mistakes are mine).

Then there are the folks whose tractors I shot for the serial number placements—Dale Onsrud, Don Paske, the inimitable (and who'd want to?) Bob Steinhorst, and Mike Kowalkowski. (I don't think I'm missing anyone.)

Information came mainly from the IH Archives in Madison (where the pages deserve thanks for putting up with me for requesting boxes over and over again); however, some very good information also came from Daryl Miller at *Red Power Magazine*.

A major thank you goes out to Lorry Dunning, who wrote the *John Deere Tractor Data Book* and who went through all these miseries first and produced the format that I followed to a degree. I can only hope that this book generates the respect (and sales) that his did.

Introduction

This book lists data for International Harvester Company (IH) wheeled tractors from the introduction of the McCormick-Deering 15-30 in 1921 to the last of the "hundred-fifty" series, the 650, which was produced until 1958. The models are listed in chronological order for the most part, although a few exceptions have been made to keep similar models together (the International A and Farmall Super A, for example, are together).

For each of the models in this book, the basic specifications have been listed. The information was chosen with the collector in mind, the concept being to bring all of the data you'd be likely to need in one, easy-to-use source. In addition to the basic serial numbers, years of production, specifications, capacities, and dimensions, you'll find serial number plate locations, Nebraska Tractor Test numbers, optional and regular equipment lists, and major engineering changes.

As a final note, those of you looking for information on early tractors, TracTracTors, IH stationary engines, and the post-1958 models, take heart. We hope to do a second volume with those models covered in the same detail you see here. It may not be published until the turn of the century, but we do know you are out there.

Where the Data Originates

The data in this book was taken from primary materials housed in the State Historical Society of Wisconsin (SHSW). This extensive collection contains an amazing amount of material, including parts and maintenance manuals for almost all tractors and implements built in the United States, and a great deal of tractors and implements produced overseas. Thousands of photographs are stored there as well as advertising materials from the 1800s up to the 1980s, although the years from 1910 up 1956 are the best represented. Paint Committee decisions have been transferred from Navistar (formerly the International Truck Division) to SHSW, covering implement and tractor paint schemes from the 1920s up to the 1950s. Yearly serial number records are there as well. What the SHSW does not have is build cards, shipping records, blueprints, and patent information. Patent information is available from your local patent library, depending on what you are looking for. Other patent information may be at the National Archives.

A Brief History of International Tractor and Engine Production

The International Harvester Company formed in 1902 as a merger of several major harvesting manufacturers. McCormick Harvester Company and the Deering Company, the largest companies in the merger, were also bitter competitors forced to combine to survive. Both had experimented with self-propelled farm equipment before they merged.

The IH corporate structure was highly complex immediately after the merger, with most parts of the merged companies operating much as they had before. Due to this, early tractor IH development took place within several different divisions, with competition between the departments nearly as zealous as it had been before the merger. The company eventually settled on two separate tractor engineering divisions who produced the Titan and Mogul lines.

The first tractor IH produced was the International Friction Drive, a combination of a chassis purchased from the Ohio Manufacturing Company and an IH horizontal stationary engine. This experiment proved to be a success, prompting IH to continue developing tractors and expand the line to include Moguls, Titans, and the Type A, B, C, and D models. Heavy and cumbersome, these early machines primary task was breaking large plots of ground and powering equipment via the belt pulley.

By 1910, IH executives started to push for smaller, cheaper, and more efficient tractors. The Mogul group produced the Mogul 12-25, Mogul 8-16, and the revolutionary but failure-prone International 8-16, while the Titan engineers brought out the Titan 12-25 and staid but reliable Titan 10-20. With these smaller tractors spearheading the model line, IH dominated the tractor market until the advent of the Fordson.

One Department, One Goal

The Mogul and Titan engineers were moved into one division in 1917, effectively ending the competition between the two staffs. At that time, the Fordson tractor was proving to be a real competitive problem for IH, and a tractor that was either cheaper or much better was needed. The answer the newly merged department came up with was the McCormick-Deering 15-30 and 10-20. These tractors had ball bearing crankshaft bearings, effective air filters, and sleeved engines, creating an extremely reliable tractor easily more capable and durable than the Fordson.

Another legendary tractor started out in 1915 as a general purpose tractor, and was marketed in 1917 and 1918 as a motor cultivator. The motor cultivator didn't work well, and was too expensive to manufacture, so the project went back to the drawing board. By 1924, after a long and arduous design process, the tractor had been radically transformed into the Farmall. First produced in significant numbers by 1926, this tractor changed the entire tractor industry with its ability to cultivate row crops, as well as perform the other tasks around the farm. The Farmall was a major innovation and is clearly the most important development in IH history.

The Farmall was modified in the 1930s to create the F-20, and enlarged to create the F-30. The McCormick-Deering 15-30 and 10-20 were also modified to produce the W-40 and W-30, although the 10-20 was produced long after its descendant started production.

A new, small line of tractors was introduced in the early 1930s. The 12 line, consisting of the F-12, W-12, I-12, O-12, and Fairway 12, was a much smaller and different line of tractors than the older line of IH tractors. Frames, engines, and transmissions were completely different from previous IH designs. The "12"-series tractors, especially the F-12, proved popular even during the Depression, and started another industry-wide trend toward producing smaller tractors.

Letter Series and Beyond

By the late 1930s, the IH line was starting to show its age. Most of the tractors' designs dated back to the early 1920s. Industrial designer Raymond Loewy was hired to redesign the entire farm tractor line, resulting in the letter-series Farmalls and the W-series conventional tractors. The A, B, H, and M were introduced in 1939, while the W-series was introduced in 1940. The letter-series tractors' low cost and attractive styling made them some of the most prolific tractors ever built, with hundreds of thousands of them sold, and they have become one of the most popular tractors collected today. The W-4, W-6, and W-9, along with their industrial and orchard versions, were also popular in certain areas and applications.

By the mid-1940s, the line of tractors began to age. Ford was offering tough competition with advanced hydraulics in smaller tractors, and Oliver's large tractors offered higher horsepower output than comparable IH machines.

The Super A and C were introduced in 1947 and 1948 to introduce hydraulics into IH's smaller tractors, which previously had exhaust-driven lifts. The Super C, Super H, and Super M were introduced in 1951 to increase the power available. In the 1950s, the small-tractor trend reversed, with more horsepower and larger machines in demand.

IH did introduce a smaller tractor in 1947, the famous Cub. The Cub was aimed at "gentleman farmers"—those who had a city job and operated a small farm part-time. Tobacco, truck, and specialized farms were also a target market for the Cub.

The Torque Amplifier tractors—the Super MTA and Super W6TA—were introduced in late 1953 and were produced only for one year. These tractors, based on the Super M and Super 6 family of tractors, introduced a planetary-gear torque amplifier (TA) that enabled a tractor to be shifted into a lower range of gears in the field while still moving. This feature added a great deal of versatility and usefulness to the tractors.

The "Hundred" Series was introduced in late 1954. This series introduced new sheet metal. The 50 and 30 Series followed shortly thereafter with other minor changes.

Tractors continued to be produced by IH until 1985, when the IH agricultural division was sold to Tenneco and merged with the Case tractor division to form Case-IH.

Understanding the Numbers

On any given tractor, at least four sets of numbers and identification codes are of importance to the collector:

1. Chassis serial number
2. Engine serial number
3. Parts numbers
4. Foundry casting date codes

In addition, there may be other numbers throughout the tractor, such as supplier's parts numbers (for parts bought outside of IH), numbers on parts indicating size and location (0.30 crankshafts, piston order, and so on), and others.

Engine and Chassis Serial Numbers

These numbers are the most familiar to collectors. The chassis serial number is usually located on a plate somewhere on the main body of the tractor, although some early IH serial numbers were stamped on the frame rails. The engine serial number is located either on a plate or is more commonly stamped on the block.

The serial number is basically the production number of that particular piece. Keep in mind, however, that a tractor bearing serial number 577 could be the 577th tractor produced, the 476th produced, or the 76th tractor produced, depending on where IH began the serial number count. Usually, IH started the numbering at number 501.

Both tractor engines and tractor chassis have their own numbers. These numbers may or may not match, depending on the tractor and year. Usually, if the numbers do not match, they are fairly close. Most of the references that IH compiled mention only the chassis serial number.

Parts Numbers

Looking more closely at the tractor, the collector will see numbers on individual parts. The numbers are either parts numbers or foundry casting codes on large, poured pieces. The parts numbers identify each individual part in order to make ordering a replacement easier, as well as to identify the part in the factory and the dealership parts bin.

The history of IH's parts numbering system is a story within itself. In the beginning, IH was composed of several companies, which came together in 1902 to form the larger company. Each company produced a line of equipment, and each company had at least one system of numbering its parts. The result was a jumbled mess. To add to the problems, IH started buying more companies with even more parts number systems.

One of the problems with the existing parts systems is that revisions, individual parts, and assemblies could not be kept separate. Eventually, prefixes and suffixes were used to identify tractor, truck, and engine parts.

To understand IH's part system, you must know the basic parts of a parts number (even the numbers have parts!). In the IH system, there are three parts to the number: prefix, number, and suffix. The prefix is the letter or letters that come before the number, such as the "G" in "G146." The basic number is the "146." A suffix is the letter or letters that come after a basic number, such as the "D" in "146 D."

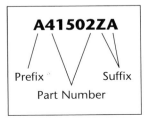

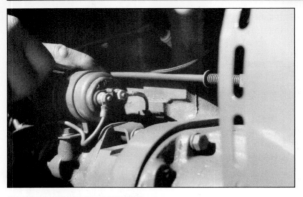

ENGINE NUMBER LOCATION
Engine numbers are considerably more difficult to find, sometimes hiding behind the ignition unit. The engine number here is on a milled, flat surface immediately to the right of the right wire coming out of the ignition coil. Bob Steinhorst is the lovely hand model.

IH used three major types of parts numbering systems over the years. The first system was used up until 1945. The second system was used in tractors, trucks, and engines in the 1930s and 1940s and is known as the "D" system of suffixes. The third system—known as the "R" system—was implemented in 1945 and gradually supplanted the earlier systems.

First-Era Parts Numbering System

The original company era of parts numbers covers the early companies and their continuation within IH. Suffixes and prefixes identified the type of machine that the part was used on, although some of the letters identified the company. In some cases, several companies used the same letter to identify different types of equipment. Other letters were retired when one line was discontinued and then used to designate something different as IH started building new machines.

To further confuse the issue, some parts started off being used in one kind of machine and then were used in another completely different kind of machine. This confusing system became completely unworkable when automated inventory systems started appearing in the 1940s. The system was gradually replaced as parts were discontinued, but a few of these old-style numbers may be rumbling around somewhere within Case-IH yet today.

Prefixes and Suffixes for Early IH Parts

Note: Plain five digit numbers were used for a variety of implements.

Code	Prefix/ Suffix	Type of Equipment
A	prefix	variety of implements

AP	prefix	Australian implements (APDAustralian discs, APW Australian wheels, APQ Australian washers, others as well)
A	suffix	cotton and corn pickers, potato planters, and potato diggers
B	prefix	grain binders, rice binders, and seeding machines
B	suffix	cultivators
C	prefix	corn binders and reapers
CM, CS	prefix	lengths of chain (CM is malleable, CS is steel)
CP	prefix	cane mills, plows, and cotton and corn pickers used in the South (mostly Chattanooga Plow company products originally)
CWK	prefix	check row wire
C	suffix	dairy equipment, including cream separators, milkers, and milk coolers (note: a C suffix followed by numbers is different and will be covered later)
D	prefix	mowers
D, DM, and DR	suffix	will be discussed in later section
E	prefix	huskers and shredders
E4 and E4A	prefix	magnetos
E	suffix	tractors, power units, and trucks
F	prefix	seeding machines and field cultivators
FP, FPJT, FPRC, FPTH, and FPW		various French company products
F	suffix	feed grinders and hammer mills
G	prefix	variety of implements as well as some parts for tractors, power units, and trucks, mainly older
G	suffix	hay loaders and fertilizer distributors
GT	suffix	tractors
H	prefix	variety of implements, also tractor, power units, and trucks, mainly binder and harvester-thresher parts
HWST	prefix	variety of implements
H1	suffix	Hough products; these numbers appeared after IH started using the R system; six-digit numbers were used during the IH years; seven digits were used after IH sold the line in 1982
H	suffix	trucks, tractors, and power units
HO	suffix	trucks
I	prefix	soil pulverizers and reapers
J	prefix	variety of implements
J	suffix	various French company products
K	prefix	hay and grain machines
K	suffix	mainly harvester-threshers, also tractors and manure spreaders
L	prefix	stationary engines, reapers, and a variety of implements
L	suffix	ensilage cutters and Ronning ensilage harvesters
M	prefix	harvester-threshers and mowers

M	suffix	seeding machines
N	prefix	grain drills
N	suffix	stationary threshers
O	prefix	plow bottoms
P and PO	prefix	implements, including harrows, listers, middle busters, planters, and plows (PO stands for Parlin & Orendorff")
P	suffix	hay presses
Q	prefix	common hardware (nuts, bolts, washers, and so on)
R	prefix	hay machines, rakes, side rakes, and tedders
RP	prefix	plows
R	suffix	cotton pickers (but not an R with a number after it)
S	prefix	variety of implements
SA	prefix	plows
SL	prefix	cultivator shovels
T	prefix	variety of implements, mainly corn shellers
TH	prefix	Ronning ensilage harvesters
T and TM	suffix	tractors, power units, and trucks (T refers probably to those parts designed by the Ed Johnston-headed team at Akron Works and the Chicago Tractor Works; TM probably refers to Milwaukee-designed tractor parts; replaced by D-suffixed parts in 1917)
U	prefix	corn pickers
UJ	suffix	universal-joint parts for harvester-threshers
V	prefix	variety of implements, usually binders
V	suffix	tractors, trucks, and power units, but mainly trucks
W	prefix	variety of implements
W	suffix	wagons, all-purpose trucks, and tractor trailers
X	prefix	variety of implements
XL	prefix	corn shellers
X	suffix	springs, except when used with other letters
Y	prefix	corn binders and corn shellers
Z	prefix	various implements
ZA	prefix	Avco-New Idea products
Z	suffix	only used with other letters

Late in the history of the "T" and "TM" tractor parts, suffix letters began to be used to denote changes in the part. For instance, if 101-T was changed, the number could become 101-TA. Some parts were originally designed by the Johnston team, but then were taken over by the Milwaukee team, and the suffix changed from T to TM. To further confuse matters, sometimes "1/3" and "1/2" numbers were used as well.

"D" Parts Numbering System

The first-era parts numbering system became especially troublesome when used with parts for tractors, trucks, engines, and power units due to frequent parts changes and common parts interchange between lines. The "D" parts numbering system was devised to handle these problems.

The "D" codes are found extensively on machinery dating from the 1920s, 1930s, 1940s, and 1950s. The "D" suffix identifies the first version of the basic part. If the basic part was changed but could still be used in place of the old part, an "A" was added to the end, ending up with "DA." Subsequent changes were in letter order, such as "DB," "DC," and so on, up to "DW."

The "D" parts numbering system was also used for parts assemblies (a group of parts sold as one set). The number for an assembly was followed by the suffix "DX." It got somewhat complicated when changes were made. If a change was made to the basic part, the part became "DAX" if the assembly was still interchangeable with the new part. If the change was made to a different part, or if different parts were added, the assembly became "DXA."

If a more complete level of assembly was desired and more parts added to a "DX" assembly, the suffix became "DY." If still more parts were added, it became a "DZ."

"R1" Parts Numbering System

The combination of increased automation, World War II production, and the pure confusion of the old parts numbering system forced IH to change its parts numbering system in March 1945.

For military production, manufacturers were required to use industry-standard parts numbers. As a result, a system devised by General Motors soon became the industry standard, which is what IH adopted.

The new system used six- and seven-digit numbers without prefixes or suffixes for "common hardware" such as nuts, bolts, screws, and other widely used parts. These parts had the same numbers across several industries, notably the auto industry.

Parts specific to IH used five-, six-, and seven-digit numbers followed by an R and either one or two digits. The first five, six, or seven digits were separated by spaces so that they were divided into groups of three, "56 809 R1," for example. The "R" section was kept separate from the rest of the number. The reasons for the separations were almost certainly for IH's new data processing systems: IBM punch cards!

There were several different layers in the "R" system. Let's use a hypothetical cylinder head, part number 555 555 R1. This would be first production version of the head. If the cylinder head was changed but was still interchangeable with the old part number, it would become 555 555 R2. Interchangeable replacements would be assigned a new R number each time they were changed, for up to eight times. After R8, the part was given a new basic part number.

Assemblies were handled in a way that the same part number could be used for the basic part and for two levels of assemblies. Changes in any of the assemblies could be covered in the R system. If 555 555 R1 was used in an assembly, such as a package including valve guides, the R number added a digit, and part number 555 555 R1 became part number 555 555 R11. The "R11" was not "R eleven" but actually "R one, one." If the basic cylinder head changed, but the rest of the assembly did not, the number became 555 555 R21. However, if the smaller parts in the assembly underwent a change, the number became 555 555 R12. This system was good up to R89.

A series of numbers for different or more complete assemblies was reserved starting at R91. If 555 555 R11 had a few more parts added to make it a complete assembly, such as a camshaft, the suffix became R91, but unlike the earlier assemblies, the basic number was changed as well. Other different types of assemblies receiving an R91 number would include an example of a cylinder head receiving a different type of valve seat than the normal assembly. Another example would be a number of parts included together as an assembly, but in which there was no predominant part, such as a set of piston rings or main-bearing caps.

The basic numbers were blocked and assigned for specific uses or engineering locations. For instance, 12 000 R1 to 49 999 R1 were always common hardware parts that were specific to the farm-implement industry and did not receive plain part numbers like the other common hardware parts that were used by the auto industry. Numbers 50 000 R1 to 994 999 R1 were used for other parts. Numbers 350 000 to 409 999 were assigned to farm tractors in the early years of the system. Numbers 995 000 R1 to 999 999 R1 were assigned to special merchandising items that could be bought by dealers, such as signs, post cards, parts racks, and thousands of others. Numbers 1 000 000 R1 to 1 017 999 R1 were assigned to packaging material, instruction books, and transfers (decals), while numbers starting with 1 030 000 R1 were assigned to shop assemblies (parts assemblies used in the factories) and shipping packages.

Casting Date Codes

Also present on certain tractors, on the larger castings, is the casting date code. The codes represent the date that the piece was cast. There are many possible reasons why IH dated the castings, but the most likely reasons are to know how long they had to season the castings (castings were left to age before machining) and to follow up on problems during production that showed up during actual use.

By reading the codes, it is possible to deduce an approximate date of manufacture. The precise date of manufacture cannot be determined, of course, due to differing lead times between casting and manufacturing, different seasoning times, and travel times between the foundry and the tractor assembly plant.

Casting codes seem to follow two formats. The first is just the straight month, date, and year (12-3-36, for example). These codes are found infrequently, seemingly without pattern, although W-30s from the mid-1930s often show this code on the engine block.

The second format is a bit more complicated. The date and month are the same, but the year is replaced by a letter, such as 12-3-F. The letter code was based at first on the normal alphabetical sequence of letters, with A equaling 1931, B equaling 1932, and so on.

FARMALL A CASTING CODE LOCATION

The A's casting codes tend to be on the right side of the tractor. The rear drive casting code is seen under the crank bracket on this tractor.

FARMALL A AND B CASTING CODE LOCATION

The location of casting codes on the Farmall As and Bs tends to be variable. This one has an engine block code located a few inches under the mag-

ENGINE BLOCK CASTING CODE LOCATION

The casting code for the Cub's block is on top next to the breather here, while the part number is underneath it. This engine is a good example of how a good thin layer of paint keeps the numbers crisp and adds to the attractiveness of the tractor.

FARMALL C CASTING CODE LOCATION

Farmall Cs have a code on the rear platform behind the clutch pedal. This one has a fairly straightforward code and part number above it. Some Cs have "USRC" cast into the platform. What it means, no one seems to know.

TORQUE TUBE CASTING CODE LOCATION

The casting code for the torque tube of this Farmall C is located to the left of the hydraulic valve (and the starter), while the part number is further to the left, next to the transmission casing, under the battery box.

LARGE FARMALL CASTING CODE LOCATION

On the larger Letter Series tractors, the casting codes are easier to find and from the clutch housing back are on the right side of the tractor. The part number is immediately right of the brake pedals, while the casting code is further right.

HYDRAULIC RESERVOIR AND CLUTCH HOUSING CASTING CODE LOCATION

On this late Super H, the hydraulic reservoir has the code on the right side, while the clutch housing casting code is directly underneath and runs vertically.

FRONT WHEEL CASTING CODE LOCATION

Wheels can be fun to find codes on, but don't forget that many of these will have dates that vary widely from the rest of the tractor. This front wheel has a casting code near the hub.

REAR WHEEL CASTING CODE LOCATION
This rear wheel has a code running on the outside, near the rim.

However, like many other things that IH did over the years, problems developed and changes occurred. One problem was that some cast letters look like numbers. Another problem was that certain letters look like certain other letters. The problems were eliminated by eliminating those letters, but in some cases, months went past before the problem was noticed and corrected. The first instance of problems appears to have taken place with the letters "U" and "V." The letter "U" was used for a few months, and then replaced with "W," and the next year "V" was replaced with "X." The author found one tractor, a W-9, where the parts had both the "U" and the "W," a sort of missing link of the tractor world.

Casting codes were not always used on earlier parts. It is very hard to find the codes on tractors built during the 1930s, for instance. The codes themselves are very small, and there are very few of them on the parts. The author has not found any codes on an F-12. F-20s have a code on the middle of the front steering bolster, on the central post where the steering post passes through. Casting codes do show up on cast wheels with some frequency.

Codes start showing up in larger numbers in 1939 with the letter-series Farmalls. Both the H and M are fairly easy to find codes on. Early As and Bs have few casting codes, with only one code located on the right front of the engine block behind the magneto. Tractors built later in the 1940s, however, tend to have more casting codes.

Codes can usually be found on belt pulley carriers (although these dates vary considerably from the other dates on the tractors), engine blocks, transmission cases, cast wheels, hydraulic pumps, clutch cases, and other parts. The location of the codes on the parts themselves wanders over the years, with the codes going from the front to the rear to the middle, for instance. The codes also appear straight up, upside down, sideways, or even slanted.

Matching Casting Date Codes with Years

Later IH casting codes are dated month, day, year, with a code for the year (12-31-F, for example). The letter codes and their corresponding year are listed below.

Letter	Year
A	1931
B	1932
C	1933
D	1934
E	1935
F	1936
G	1937
H	1938
I	1939
J	1940
K	1941
L	1942
M	1943
N	1944
O	1945
P	1946
Q	1947
R	1948
S	1949
T	1950
U	1951
W	1951
X	1952
Y	1953
Z	1954
A	1955
B	1956
C	1957
D	1958

In later years, even more letters were dropped, although U was reinstated. Code letters I, O, Q, V, and Z were dropped. Code letter B was later dropped. The exact years that each letter was dropped are unknown, making the codes difficult to predict.

X Codes

Tractors from about 1939 to sometime in the 1950s used a combination letter and number suffix code to indicate options. The codes seem to be the same from tractor to tractor, although of course not every code was used on a particular tractor. The codes opened with a letter, X for Farmalls, W for W-series tractors, or Y for industrial tractors. It would be wonderful to identify which codes are valid for each tractor, but the build cards are long gone, and the parts manuals list codes that seemingly would not apply to that tractor, such as a cotton-harvester code in the Cub manual or the I-4 transmission codes in the W-9 manual.

A few of these codes also apply to crawler tractors, but most crawler codes are actually quite different, referring to track equipment.

In the following list, ignore the first letter:

Code	Meaning
X1	gasoline
X1A	gasoline, low-speed gears
X1B	gasoline, 5,000-foot altitude
X1C	gasoline, 8,000-foot altitude
X1D	pneumatic tires, swinging drawbar
X1E	gasoline, 5,000-foot altitude, low-speed gears
X1F	gasoline, high-speed gears
X1G	gasoline, high-speed gears, low-speed gears
X1H	gasoline, high-speed gears, 8,000-foot altitude
X1J	gasoline, 7-mph high-speed gears, 5,000-foot altitude
W1K	battery ignition, hydraulic pump drive, starting, and lighting
X1L	gasoline, 7-mph high-speed gears, low-low-speed gears, 5,000- foot altitude
X1M	gasoline, 8,000-foot altitude, low-low-speed gears
X1N	gasoline, 8,000-foot altitude, low-low-speed gears, 7-mph high-speed gears
X2	modified
Y2A	modified, 5,000-foot altitude
Y2B	modified, high-speed reverse
X3	kerosene
X3A	kerosene, low-speed gears
X3B	kerosene, 5,000-foot altitude
X3C	kerosene, 8,000-foot altitude
X3D	kerosene, high-speed gears
W3E	7-mph high-speed gears
W3F	I-4 transmission
X3G	kerosene, 7-mph high-speed gears, 5,000-foot altitude
X3H	kerosene, 7-mph high-speed gears, low-low-speed gears
X4	shop mule
X5	5,000-foot altitude
X5A	5,000-foot altitude, 7-mph high-speed gears
X6	low-speed gears
X6A	low-speed gears
X6B	low-speed gears
X6C	low-speed gears
X8	8,000-foot altitude

X9	high-speed gears
X10	10,000-foot altitude
X11	engines with undersized crankshaft
X11S	engines with undersized crankshaft (service)
W12	pneumatic tires
W12A	pneumatic tires, swinging drawbar
W12B	pneumatic tires, swinging drawbar, starting, and lighting
W12C	pneumatic tires, swinging drawbar
W13	swinging drawbar
W13A	swinging drawbar, starting, or lighting
X14	starting or lighting
X14A	battery ignition with starting or lighting and adjustable front axle
Y15	U.S. Army Air Corps
W16	over-center hand-operated clutch
X17	distillate
X17A	distillate, 5,000-foot altitude
X17D	distillate, 8,000-foot altitude
X18	unlisted feature
X19	special transmission
X20	cotton harvester
X20A	cotton harvester, gasoline
X20B	cotton harvester, kerosene
X20C	cotton harvester, diesel
X21	7-mph high-speed gears, 8,000-foot altitude
X22	adjustable front axle (heavy duty)
X22A	adjustable front axle
X23	Auburn clutch
X24	nonadjustable front axle

Chassis and Engine Alphabets

An alternative to the X, Y, and W codes were single-letter suffixes. IH seems to have used these after the X, W, and Y codes in the 1950s, but a note on the IH archive's listing indicates that these codes were used from 1939 on. These codes were used at least into the 1960s.

Code	Meaning
A	distillate
B	kerosene
C	LPG
D	5,000-foot altitude
E	8,000-foot altitude
F	cotton picker mounting attachment (high drum)
G	cotton picker tractor attachment (high drum)
H	rear frame cover and shifter attachment
I	Rockford clutch
J	Rockford clutch

K	optional 4th gear
L	high-altitude cylinder head
M	low-speed attachment
N	LPG-burning attachment (2,500 feet and up)
O	na
P	independent PTO attachment without TA
Q	na
R	TA with provision for transmission-driven PTO
S	TA with provision for 540 independent PTO
T	cotton picker mounting attachment (low drum)
U	high-altitude attachment (gas and LPG fuels)
V	exhaust-valve rotator
W	forward and reverse drive
X	high-speed low and reverse attachment
Y	Hydra Touch low and reverse attachment (with 12-gpm pump)
Z	Hydra Touch power supply (with 17-gpm pump)
AA	1,000-rpm independent PTO drive
BB	na
CC	third-speed heavy-duty tillage gear
EE	na
FF	hydraulic power supply with 4.5-gpm pump
GG	hydraulic power supply with 7.0-gpm pump
HH	no provision for PTO
II	na
JJ	na
KK	optional 4th gear
LL	increased-speed low-gear attachment
MM	na
NN	hydraulic power supply (Farmall tractor only with 17- and 9-gpm pump)
OO	
PP	high-capacity hydraulic power supply (IH tractor only)

IH Engine Suffix Alphabet

Code	Meaning
A	distillate-burning attachment
B	kerosene-burning attachment
C	LPG-burning attachment
D	5,000-foot-altitude attachment
E	8,000-foot-altitude attachment
F	na
G	na
HA	high-altitude cylinder heads
I	na
J	na
K	cast-iron pistons

23

L	high-altitude cylinder heads
M	na
N	LPG attachment (2,500 feet and up)
O	na
P	na
Q	na
R	exhaust-valve-rotator attachment
S	na
T	na
U	high-altitude attachment
V	exhaust-valve-rotator attachment

Serial Numbers Versus Numbers Produced

With International Harvester, a book like this is a pretty miserable project to do. IH never kept records that were terribly consistent when it came to tractors. The most noticeable problem is with serial numbers and numbers of tractors produced: rarely does anything match up. There are several reasons for this.

IH records show tractors produced and serial numbers by years. For example, records show that IH built 6,150 Farmall 200s in 1956 with the serial numbers 10904–15698. Simple enough, right?

Where things get confusing is how IH defines a "year." The calendar year (January 1–December 31) was used quite frequently but so was the "fiscal year" which, for IH, lasted from November 1 to October 31. Also, there is the "season" which was used for the very earliest tractors and basically ran from when the factories started building tractors (sometimes in October, sometimes in November, sometimes other months) to when they stopped building tractors for that planting season (sometimes in March, sometimes later).

Which "year" IH used for what also changed over the years. For instance, with serial numbers the season was apparently used up until the late 1910s, followed by the fiscal year. Eventually, serial numbers went to calendar years (apparently with the Letter Series tractors in 1939, but this could have happened later). While it is not totally clear what "year" IH used for numbers produced, they likely used fiscal years, except on government reports, which contain calendar years. The problems between serial numbers and production numbers, as far as years, is the worst in the 1950s, where, for the Hundreds and the 50s, IH listed serial numbers in some years but no production numbers. In this book, the extra year is added in the production numbers, where appropriate.

If you do the math, chassis serial numbers do not add up to the same numbers as production numbers in most cases. There are many reasons for this. The simplest is that for later tractors, the serial number plates came from an outside manufacturer with the sequential number pre-stamped, and sometimes, plates were lost or destroyed because of damage.

Other causes of differences were tractors with serial numbers that were returned to the factory, dismantled, and then deducted from the numbers produced. Other tractors were produced for original equipment manufacturers (OEMs) and were assigned serial numbers but were not officially considered tractors. In other cases tractors may have been considered built but then not assigned a serial number. In a few cases, experimental tractors may have been counted as tractors produced but may have had serial numbers in a different series.

Multiple Serial Number Lists

In some cases, IH recorded two or three different sets of serial numbers for the same tractor. Rather than decide for you which is correct, both sets are given. In a few cases, the serial numbers have been checked against real live tractors with casting codes (notably the -6 Series). It seems that the higher serial numbers are more accurate, but there may be exceptions. Always double check the serial number against the casting codes if there is a question.

In the case of engine serial numbers, both service engines (replacement engines) and engines for other purposes may have been taken from the regular sequence of numbers.

Dimensions and Weights

Dimensions and weights are variables dependent on several different factors. Wheel and tire equipment is the major variable. Different sizes can change length, width, height, and weight. Front axles are another example. Farmalls could and did have wide front axles or narrow front axles, which changed all of the above dimensions as well. Of course, various options such as wheel weights, special wide axles, hydraulics, air pipe extensions, etc., all change the dimensions. Take the dimension listings in the book as a rough guide. The advertising department was also in the practice of rounding off numbers, occasionally resulting in as many as three slightly different versions of the same dimension.

Regular Equipment and Equipment

Special equipment is a category that's fairly easy to understand. It's the stuff that could be ordered from IH to put on your tractor, either at the factory or, in many cases, at the dealership or your own shop. However, by the early 1950s, IH was packaging its tractors with special options for sales purposes, mainly as a way of predicting sales and production better and also to assist sales. Many "options" for tractors in the 1950s were actually found on nearly all those produced.

Regular equipment is a bit more difficult to trace. The term "regular equipment" was more of an advertising term, and the information within on regular equipment is taken from advertising literature. Often, the buyer was given a choice of certain wheels, lugs, or tires as part of the base tractor. In fact, IH tended to sell four or five different packages for each individual model rather than one base tractor to which all options had to be added.

The difficult part is that special equipment tended to become regular equipment over the years and vice versa. Special equipment was also added over the years, thus the special equipment sections do not refer to any one year but rather the entire production run.

To further confuse the issue, IH produced special equipment and entire versions of the tractors for either large customers or very specialized operations. Sometimes, the company did not want to advertise the existence of this equipment to other potential buyers due to expense, so these became known as "unlisted features," a few of which are mentioned (a complete listing of these unlisted features does not currently exist).

Finally, lacking is a complete listing of all the tires, wheels, lugs, rims, and other things that go on the ends of axles to connect the tractor with the ground. The variety that IH offered was staggering. IH manufactured its own equipment for some of these items and dealt with other companies (French & Hecht, Goodyear, Goodrich, and a host of others) for more parts.

TRACTOR DATA

McCormick-Deering 15-30 Gear-Drive Orchard, Orchard California, and Orchard Low Wheel

Engine	inline, removable sleeves, ball bearings
Cylinders	four
Bore and stroke	4 1/2x6 inches
Displacement	381 cubic inches
Rated rpm	1,000
Compression ratio	na
Ignition	magneto
Carburetor	1-inch Ensign Type JTW
Cooling capacity	14 gallons
Fuel tank capacity	18 gallons fuel, 1 gallon starting, 9 gallons water for water injection system
Horsepower ratings	
Drawbar	15
PTO/belt	30
Length	137 inches
Wheelbase	85 inches
Height	70 inches
Width	65 inches
Available treads	52 inches (front), 53 inches (rear)
Weight	5,800 pounds (shipping weight)

Speed

Gear	Speed
1	2 mph
2	3 mph
3	4 mph
Reverse	2 3/4 mph

Price ....na

Nebraska test number....................................87 and 130

Numbers produced

1921	199
1922	1,350
1923	4,886
1924	7,321
1925	12,978
1926	20,001
1927	17,554
1928	35,525
1929	28,311

MCCORMICK-DEERING 15-30 GEAR DRIVE
The McCormick-Deering 15-30 Gear Drive was initially introduced in 1921 as the International 15-30 Gear Drive, becoming a McCormick-Deering in 1923 when it entered full production. The tractor has a deeper gasoline tank than its little brother, the McCormick-Deering 10-20 Gear Drive. Both of these tractors were excellent for their day and played a very large part in the sales victory over the Fordson. *State Historical Society of Wisconsin*

Serial numbers

1921	112–310
1922	311–1660
1923	1661–6546
1924	6547–13867
1925	13868–26845
1926	26846–48646
1927	46847–64400
1928	64401–99925
1929	na
Chassis prefixes	TG
Engine prefixes	TG
Chassis serial number location	first located on fender, then moved to fuel tank support
Engine serial number location	na

Regular Equipment
Informations not available

Attachments and Special Features
Informations not available

Major Changes/Dates
Informations not available

Comments
Waukesha produced the IH 15-30 engine until 1923

McCormick-Deering Gear-Drive 10-20

Engine	inline, removable sleeves, ball bearings
Cylinders	four
Bore and stroke	4 1/4x5 inches
Displacement	284 cubic inches
Rated rpm	1,000
Compression ratio	na
Ignition	Splitdorf 46C Aero magneto (1923–1926), IH E4A magneto (1925 and on), or Robert Bosch ZU-4 magneto (special)
Carburetor	1 1/4-inch Ensign JH (1923) or 1 1/4-inch Ensign Type JA (1923–end of production)
Cooling capacity	10 gallons
Fuel tank capacity	14 1/2 gallons, 3/4 gallons starting

Horsepower ratings

Drawbar	10

28

MCCORMICK-DEERING 10-20, 15-30, AND W-30
SERIAL NUMBER LOCATION

Early IH wheel tractors, such as the McCormick-Deering 10-20, 15-30, and W-30, have the chassis serial number plate mounted on the forward gas tank support.

PTO/belt	20
Length	123 inches
Wheelbase	na
Height	62 inches
Width	60 inches
Available treads	na
Weight	3,925 pounds (shipping weight)

Speed

Gear	Speed
1	2 mph (1924), 2 1/4 mph (1935)
2	3 mph
3	4 mph (1924), 4 1/4 mph (1935)
Reverse	2 3/4 mph (1924), 2 mph (1935)

Price	$850 (1924)
Nebraska test number	95 and 142

Numbers produced

1923	7,117
1924	11,197
1925	18,436
1926	25,021
1927	26,646
1928	30,353
1929	39,433
1930–39	na

Serial numbers

1923	501–7640
1924	7641–18868
1925	18869–19000, 19100–24999, and 25125–37727
1926	37728–45000 and 45076–62823
1927	62824–89469
1928	89470–119822
1929	119823–159110 and 159651–159796
1930	159111–191485 (except 159651–159796)
1931	191486–201012 and 201801–203174
1932	201013–201800 and 203175–204238
1933	none built
1934	204239–206178
1935	206179–207274
1936	207275–210234
1937	210235–212424
1938	212425–214885
1939	214886–215973

Chassis prefixes .... KC
Engine prefixes .... KCE
Chassis suffixes (after KC 204239)

P	pneumatic tires
M	modified
SP	four-speed transmission
HA	high-altitude pistons
S	special attachment
NT	narrow tread (see 10-20 narrow-tread section)

Engine suffixes .... na
Chassis serial number location .... on plate on fuel tank support
Engine serial number location .... na

Regular Equipment
    Informations not available

Attachments and Special Features
    PTO, electric lighting, gas lighting, belt pulleys of various sizes, cushion seat, wood-rim steering wheel, low intake pipe, orchard fenders, low seat, low steering wheel, swinging drawbar, spark arrester, overhead exhaust pipe, pneumatic tires, various wheel and lug equipment, fender with apron (orchard tractor), and disc wheels (orchard tractor)

Major Changes/Dates

Production authorized January 20, 1922, and reauthorized December 29, 1922

Rice-field 10-20 authorized April 9, 1923

Location of nameplate moved from top of left fender to side of fender June 26, 1923, engine 4302, moved to center of hood sheet-rear tractor KC-4557, authorized July 16, 1923

Fuel tank reversed; authorized July 26, 1923; first used on tractor KC 3963 (unknown production date)

Special rice-field transmission with adjustable bearings first produced March 29, 1930, on tractor KC 180195

Comments

The 10-20 provided the backbone of IH's tractor marketing until 1928, and was the main "Fordson fighter." The various versions remained in production until 1940, receiving updates similar to those applied to the W-30 (the W-30 was designed to replace the 10-20 but ended up being a concurrent addition to the line). IH used the basic 10-20 platform to produce a wide array of industrial, orchard, and other special tractors. The orchards were especially different, often being produced to match the needs of a specific area or customer. Some orchard tractors got four-speed transmissions, while a few got T-20 TracTracTor manifolds and W-30 steering!

10-20 Orchards

10-20 Orchard
10-20 Orchard California
10-20 Modified Orchard (regular tread, three-speed)
10-20 Modified Orchard NT three-speed
10-20 Modified Orchard NT four-speed
10-20 Orchard (Low Seat)
10-20 Rice-field

There appear to be three separate generations of 10-20 Orchards. The first generation included the 10-20 Orchard and the 10-20 Orchard California, which were produced starting in 1923, and lasting until 1938.

The 10-20 Orchard California was shipped minus the belt pulley and shafts, and the long air pipe. The regular pulley carrier was used, but the hole for the pulley shaft was covered by a plate. The Orchard California included 5-inch spade lugs, lower steering wheel, lower seat, 3-inch-high front tire ring, and the short intake air pipe brace. A spark arrester was included, and an industrial tractor clutch housing cover was used. The fenders completely enclosed the upper half of the rear wheels. The first tractor produced was KC 13564, sometime in March 1924.

The Regular 10-20 Orchard was shipped with the belt pulley disassembled from the tractor. It also did not include the long air pipe but did include the short air intake pipe brace, 3-inch-high front wheel skid ring, low seat, and low steering wheel.

The second generation included the 10-20 Modified Orchards, a group of three tractors: 10-20 Modified Orchard with regular tread and three-speed, 10-20 Modified Orchard with narrow tread and three-speed, and 10-20 Modified Orchard with narrow tread and four-speed; these tractors were also referred to as "Jacksonville" tractors, as this was the original market they were created for. These tractors were produced beginning in late 1936 into 1938. In late 1938, IH consolidated the two different generations (five models total) into the 10-20 Orchard (Low Seat), which was based off of the Modified Orchards.

The Modified Orchards can be identified by having W-30 parts (Front Bolster 2505-D, Steering Post 2488-D, and other steering parts). The regular 10-20 front axle was used, but the stop lugs were removed. The engine had a #20 TracTracTor engine improvement package added, including the exhaust manifold (2298 DAX), intake manifold (2302 DX), and carburetor (21950-DB). The left hood was reworked to include the new parts.

The 10-20 Orchard (Low Seat) will be similar to the Modifieds, but will be after serial number KC 214814, built October 14, 1938. These tractors will also have a W-30 front axle. All 10-20 Orchards built after 214814 should be 10-20 Orchard (Low Seat) model tractors. These tractors were available with three- or, for pneumatic tires, four-speeds, and also had a T-20 Orchard-type air filter-top.

McCormick-Deering 10-20 Narrow Tread (NT)

Engine	inline, removable sleeves, ball bearings
Cylinders	four
Bore and stroke	4 1/4x5 inches
Displacement	284 cubic inches
Rated rpm	na
Compression ratio	na
Ignition	see McCormick-Deering 10-20 listing
Carburetor	na
Cooling capacity	10 gallons
Fuel tank capacity	14 1/2 gallons, 3/4 gallon starting
Horsepower ratings	
Drawbar	10
PTO/belt	20
Length	123 inches
Wheelbase	78 inches
Height	62 inches
Width	48 inches
Available treads	na
Weight	3,700 pounds (shipping weight, approximate)

Speed

    Gear ....*Speed*

    1 ....2 mph

    2 ....3 mph

    3 ....4 mph

    Reverse ....2 1/2 mph

Price ....na

Nebraska test number...................................na

Numbers produced

    1925 8

    1926 148

    1927 183

    1928 323

    1929 388

    1930–34 ....na

Serial numbers

    1925 ....na

    1926 501–648

    1927 649–831

    1928 832–1154

    1929 1155–1542

    1930 1543–1749

    1931 1750–1832

    1932 1833–1911

    1933 1912–1951

    1934 1952–1960

Chassis prefixes ....NT until 1934

Engine prefixes...............................NT

Chassis suffixes ....na

    P ....pneumatic tires

    M..modified

    SP ....four-speed transmission

    HA...high-altitude piston

    S ....special attachment

    NT...narrow tread (see 10-20 narrow-tread section; after 1934, narrow treads were included in regular 10-20 listing, and suffix NT was added)

Engine suffixes...............................na

Chassis serial number location ....on plate on fuel-tank support

Engine serial number location.....................na

Regular Equipment

    Fenders, open-type wheels; see McCormick-Deering 10-20 for rest of list

Attachments and Special Features

Special for 10-20: aprons for rear wheels, PTO, pulley, disc wheels front and rear, 10-inch-wide rear wheels (reduces width to 46 inches), spark arrester, foot brake, high skid rings; see regular McCormick-Deering 10-20 list for other options

Major Changes/Dates

Narrow-tread attachment authorized March 15, 1925

Separate 10-20 narrow tread authorized February 4, 1926; first tractor, NT 501, built February 3, 1926

Front stay rod 12839-D added to reduce turning radius on tractor NT 1521, September 23, 1929

Comments

None

Model 20 Industrial

Engine	inline, removable sleeves, ball bearings
Cylinders	four
Bore and stroke	4 1/4x5 inches
Displacement	284 cubic inches
Rated rpm	1,000
Compression ratio	na
Ignition	Splitdorf 46C Aero magneto (1923–1926), IH E4A magneto (1926 and on), or Robert Bosch ZU-4 magneto (special)
Carburetor	1 1/4-inch Ensign Type JA (1923) or Holley No. 351 (1924 and on)
Cooling capacity	10 gallons
Fuel tank capacity	24 gallons or 14 gallons (early)
Horsepower ratings	
Drawbar	na
PTO/belt	20
Length	118 inches
Wheelbase	78 inches
Height	62 inches
Width	59 inches
Available treads	52 inches (front), 62 inches (rear with double pneumatic tires, center to center)
Weight	5,480 pounds (shipping weight)
Speed	

Gear	Speed
1	2 mph
2	4 mph

MCCORMICK-DEERING 10-20 INDUSTRIAL

The McCormick-Deering 10-20 Industrial was known by several different names during its 17-year production run. However, it was sold to dozens of aftermarket producers who converted the tractor and to hundreds of other companies who made equipment that could be added to it. Here is a 10-20 Industrial with a front-mounted cable laying device. *State Historical Society of Wisconsin*

3	10 mph
4	na
Reverse	3.8 mph
Price	$1,125 (1926)
Nebraska test number	na
Numbers produced	
1923	23
1924	31
1925	328
1926	1,300
1927	1,842
1928	3,048
1929	4,607
1930–40	na
Serial numbers	
1923–1925	see McCormick-Deering 10–20 list
1925	IND 32605–32699 (different 1925 prefix)
1926	45001–45075
1926	IN 1053–2182 (different 1926 prefix)

1927	2183–4024
1928	4025–7072
1929	7073–11679
1930	11680–15076
1931	15077–16907
1932	16908–17622
1933	17623–17828
1934	17829–18037
1935	18038–18210
1936	18211–18405
1937	18406–18617
1938	18618–18737
1939	18738–18864
1940	18865–18896
Chassis prefixes	KC, IND, IN, and SIN
Engine prefixes	KCE, INE, IND, and SIN
Chassis suffixes	
B	belt pulley
D	dump body
L	differential lock
M	modified
P	pneumatic tires
S	electric starting or starting and lighting
W	farm transmission
Engine suffixes	na
Chassis serial number location	nameplate on rear hood sheet
Engine serial number location	na

Regular Equipment

Information not available

Attachments and Special Features

Electric headlights, generator, battery, belt pulley, PTO, pneumatic tires, tire pump, air brake compressor, and a variety of other wheel and tire equipment (narrow-tread available as well)

Major Changes/Dates

Twenty-five sets of solid cast disc front and rear wheels for industrial users authorized March 16, 1923

Main frame changed from 828-DD to 2074-D on tractor IN 15334, built December 15, 1930

Comments

The 10-20 Industrial tractor changed almost yearly up to the late 1920s, and in fact the collector may be challenged to find two alike, unless some large customer ordered several at once and then sold them together. There are many subvariants, such as the "New York Snow Plow Tractors," and many tractors were purchased by outside manufacturers to base their product on. The 10-20 Industrial could be a book in itself, and in fact IH did produce such a book for its industrial salesmen. The 10-20 Industrial, known also as the Model 20 Industrial and the McCormick-Deering Industrial Tractor, varied from the agricultural model in having rubber-tired disc wheels (spring-mounted in front), foot accelerator, internal expanding foot brakes, muffler, and different transmission.

McCormick-Deering 15-30 (22-36)

Engine	inline, removable sleeves, ball bearings
Cylinders	four
Bore and stroke	4 3/4x6 inches
Displacement	425 cubic inches
Rated rpm	1,000
Compression ratio	na
Ignition	IH E4A magneto or Splitdorf 46C Aero magneto; Robert Bosch FU-4-AR-S60 optional
Carburetor	1-inch IH RW
Cooling capacity	14 gallons
Fuel tank capacity	**19 gallons, 3/4 gallon starting, 9 gallons water injection**

Horsepower ratings

Drawbar	22
PTO/belt	36
Length	137 inches
Wheelbase	85 inches
Height	70 inches
Width	65 inches
Available treads	52 inches (front), 53 inches (rear)
Weight	6,540 pounds (shipping weight)

Speed

Gear	Speed
1	2 mph
2	3 1/4 mph
3	3 3/4 mph
Reverse	2 3/4 mph

Price	$1,250 (1924)
Nebraska test number	156
Numbers produced	na

Serial numbers

1929	99926–128236
1930	128237–150127
1931	150128–154507
1932	154508–156212

1933	none built; serial number skip
1934	156301–157477
Chassis prefixes	TG
Engine prefixes	TG
Chassis suffixes	
M	not known, probably indicates 22-36
MB	new-type ball bearing transmission
Engine suffixes	na
Chassis serial number location	plate on center of rear hood sheet
Engine serial number location	na

Regular Equipment
Information not available

Attachments and Special Features
Information not available

Major Changes/Dates
Information not available

Comments
None

McCormick-Deering 15-30 Orchard, Orchard California, and Orchard Low Wheel

Engine	inline, removable sleeves, ball bearings
Cylinders	four
Bore and stroke	
1921–1929	4 1/2x6 inches
1929–1934	4 3/4x6 inches
Displacement	425 or 381 cubic inches
Rated rpm	1,050
Compression ratio	na
Ignition	see McCormick-Deering 15-30 listing
Carburetor	see McCormick-Deering 15-30 listing
Cooling capacity	14 gallons
Fuel tank capacity	19 gallons kerosene, 3/4-gallon gas starting
Horsepower ratings	na
Length	na
Wheelbase	na
Height	na
Width	na
Available treads	na
Weight	na

Speed ....na
Price ....na
Nebraska test number.....................................na
Numbers produced...na
Serial numbers ....see 15-30 and 22-36 listings
Chassis prefixes ....TG
Engine prefixes...TG
Chassis suffixes..na
Engine suffixes..na
Chassis serial number location ....nameplate on rear of hood
Engine serial number location......................na

Regular Equipment
    Information not available

Attachments and Special Features
    Information not available

Major Changes/Dates
    Information not available

Comments
    None

McCormick-Deering 15-30 Industrial, International 15-30 Industrial

Engine..inline, removable sleeves, ball bearings
Cylinders ....four
Bore and stroke
1921–1929 ....4 1/2x6 inches
1929–1934 ....4 3/4x6 inches
Displacement
1921–1929 ....381 cubic inches
1929–1934 ....425 cubic inches
Rated rpm ....na
Compression ratio..na
Ignition..IH E4A magneto (regular); Splitdorf 46C Aero, Robert Bosch FU-4-AR-S60 (special)
Carburetor...1-inch IH RW
Cooling capacity ....14 gallons
Fuel tank capacity ....na
Horsepower ratings..na
Length..na
Wheelbase...na
Height ....na
Width ....na

Available treads ....na
Weight ....na
Speed..na
Price ....na
Nebraska test number.......................................na
Numbers produced...na
Serial numbers
   1930..501–548
   1931..549–874
   1932..875–1032
Chassis prefixes ....HD, HDS, and HDB
Engine prefixes...HD
Chassis serial number location ....plate on center of rear hood sheet
Engine serial number location........................na

Regular Equipment
Information not available

Attachments and Special Features
Information not available

Major Changes/Dates
Information not available

Comments
As far as serial numbers, production, etc., this may be the most confusing situation IH ever produced. At first, 15-30s were modified into industrial configurations and were included in the normal 15-30 production figures. Later, in 1930, IH produced a small run of Industrial-30 tractors, which the above data applies to. After the Model 30 ceased production in 1932, at least a few 15-30s (22-36s) were modified for industrial use and included in the 22-36 production figures.

Farmall Regular, Regular Narrow Tread, and Fairway

Engine...inline, removable sleeves
Cylinders ....four
Bore and stroke...3 3/4x5 inches
Displacement ....220 cubic inches
Rated rpm 1,200
Compression ratio...na
Ignition...IH E4A (after 1926) or Splitdorf 46C magneto (1924–1926); Robert Bosch ZU-4 magneto (special order)
Carburetor..1-inch Ensign type 3-DA-600f
Cooling capacity ....na
Fuel tank capacity ....13 gallons, 7/8 gallons starting

FARMALL REGULAR

The Farmall Regular was first produced in 1924, although it didn't get into full production until late in 1926. The tractor dominated the market by 1929 and remains the most important tractor in history, influencing every other major tractor company in the United States. The Regular can be distinguished by the exhaust under the manifold, although some have been refitted with F-20 vertical exhausts. *State Historical Society of Wisconsin*

Horsepower ratings	na
Length	123 inches
Wheelbase	85 inches
Height	67 inches (at top of steering wheel)
Width	86 inches
Available treads	74 inches (rear), 10 inches (front)
Weight	3,825 pounds

Speed

Gear	Speed
1	2 mph
2	3 mph
3	4 mph
Reverse	2 mph

Price	na
Nebraska test number	117

Numbers produced

1924	200
1925	838
1926	4,430
1927	9,502

1928	24,899
1929	35,517
1930–32	na

Serial numbers

1924	QC 501–700
1925	701–1538
1926	1539–5957 (QC 3680–3704 and 5933–5957 were narrow treads)
1927	T 5969–15470
1928	15471–40369
1929	40370–75690
1929	IT 501–696 (modified, probably industrials)
1930	75691–117783
1931	117784–131871
1932	131872–134954
Chassis prefixes	QC, T, and IT
Engine prefixes	QC, T, and IT

Chassis suffixes (after T 78405)

N	narrow tread
NW	narrow tread with wide front axle
F	fairway
S	modified
W	regular tractor with wide front axle
Engine suffixes	na
Chassis serial number location	nameplate on tool box under fuel tank
Engine serial number location	na

Regular Equipment

PTO

Attachments and Special Features

Skeleton rear wheels, fenders, orchard fenders, cotton shields, golf course wheels, cushion seat, and a variety of other wheel, lug, and rim equipment

Major Changes/Dates

First tractor, QC 501, built December 26, 1923; production of 1924 Farmalls finished February 12, 1924

First 1925 Farmall, with massive improvements, QC 701, built October 6, 1924; 1925 Farmall production finished February 21, 1925

Narrow tread first available May 5, 1927

Total of 402 tractors made with malleable iron countershaft housings (1523-DC) instead of cast steel, beginning with T 35426 (August 10, 1928) and ending with 35827

Increased-strength front bolster (1556-DD) first used June 6, 1928, on T-29996

Seat spring and bracket redesigned (1931-D Seat Support Bracket, 10214-D Seat Spring, 17399-D Seat Support), first used on tractor T 100100, built April 4, 1930

Comments

Several IH references make note of Industrial Farmall Regulars, fitted with street sweepers and similar implements. Production was most likely in the hundreds, although no separate serial number series has been found. Presumably, the "IT" refers to the industrial Farmalls.

McCormick-Deering WA-40, W-40, and WK-40

Engine	inline
Cylinders	6
Bore and stroke	3 3/4x4 inches
Displacement	298 cubic inches
Rated rpm	1,750
Compression ratio	na
Ignition	IH F-6 magneto
Carburetor	Zenith 50 AY-12 (WTM 501-up) or Zenith K5S (WTM 501–831)
Cooling capacity	12 gallons
Fuel tank capacity	31 gallons, 1 1/4 gallons starting
Horsepower ratings	
Drawbar	37.79 (max), 28.34 (rated, 75 percent of max) (IH)
PTO/belt	52.70 (max), 44.80 (rated, 85 percent of max) (IH)
Length	141 inches
Wheelbase	85 inches
Height	71 inches (at top of steering wheel)
Width	65 3/4 inches
Available treads	52 1/4 inches (front), 53 inches (rear)
Weight	6,630 pounds (shipping weight)
Speed	
Gear	*Speed (steel wheels; air tires)*
1	2 1/8 mph; 2 3/8 mph
2	2 3/4 mph; 3 mph
3	3 3/4 mph; 4 mph
4	4 3/8 mph; 12 mph
Reverse	2 3/4 mph; 3 mph
Price	$1,305 (1940, steel wheels), $1,640 (1940, pneumatic tires)
Nebraska test number	268 and 269
Numbers produced	na
Serial numbers	
1935	501–1440
1936	1441–5119

1937 5120–7664
1938 7665–9755
1939 9756–10322
1940 10323–10599
Chassis prefixes ....WAC (WA-40) and WAKC (WK-40)
Engine prefixes..WTM (WA-40) and WKE (WK-40)
Chassis serial number location ....plate on rear hood sheet
Engine serial number location........................na

Regular Equipment
Belt pulley, IH magneto, variable-speed governor, adjustable drawbar, front drawbar, manifold heat control, radiator shutter and heat control, and hand brake

Attachments and Special Features
PTO, alternative belt pulleys, waterproof upholstered seat, electric lighting and starting equipment, sliding drawbar, spark arrester, exhaust muffler, exhaust extension pipe, pneumatic tires, high-speed 4th gear for pneumatic-tired tractors (12-mph), spark plug tire pump, extension tires, and a variety of lugs and wheel equipment

Major Changes/Dates
Heavier front axle (28681-D), hubs, and knuckles first used on tractor WAC 934, produced September 20, 1935; also new transmission at that tractor and date

W-40 tractors fitted with 3 3/4x4 kerosene engines to be known as WK-40, reported effective August 27, 1936

WK-40 transmission changed to accommodate increase in rpm (from 1,600 to 1,750), produced December 2, 1936

WA-40 discontinued January 8, 1937, due to regular engines operating on both kerosene and gasoline

Comments
None

McCormick-Deering WD-40

Engine ....diesel, inline, gasoline start
Cylinders ....four
Bore and stroke..4 3/4x6 inches
Displacement ....355 cubic inches
Rated rpm 1,200
Compression ratio 17:1
Ignition..IH F-4 magneto
Carburetor..1 1/4-inch IH Model R (engine WDC 508–WDC 2176) or IH C12 (engine WDC 2177- up)
Cooling capacity ....14 gallons

Fuel tank capacity ....31 gallons
Horsepower ratings
    Drawbar...37.32 (max), 27.99 (rated, 75 percent of max)
    PTO/belt ....51.81 (max), 44.04 (rated, 85 percent of max)
Length...141 1/2 inches
Wheelbase......................................85 inches
Height ....71 inches (at top of steering wheel)
Width ....65 3/4 inches
Available treads ....52 1/4 inches (front), 53 inches (rear)
Weight ....7,550 pounds (shipping weight)
Speed

Gear	Speed (steel wheels; air tires)
1	2 3/8 mph; 2 mph
2	3 mph; 3 1/4 mph
3	4 mph; 4 1/4 mph
4	4 5/8 mph; 12 1/8 mph
Reverse	3 mph; 3 1/8 mph

Price ....$2,210 (steel wheels, 1940) or $2,516.50 (pneumatic tires, 1940)
Nebraska test number...................246
Numbers produced.........................na
Serial numbers ....see W-40 listing
Chassis prefixes ....WDC
Engine prefixes...............................WDC or WDCE
Chassis suffixes
    M...modified
    S ....special attachment
    P ....pneumatic tires
    SP ....high-speed transmission
    U...special transmission
Engine suffixes................................na
Chassis serial number location ......plate on rear hood sheet
Engine serial number location........na

Regular Equipment

Precision diesel injection pump, variable-speed governor, seven-stage fuel filtering, gasoline starting, adjustable drawbar, radiator shutter and heat indicator, belt pulley, fenders, and front drawbar

Attachments and Special Features

PTO, electric lighting, special wheel and lug equipment, belt pulleys, spark arrester, sliding drawbar, pneumatic tires, transmission for use with pneumatic tires, exhaust muffler, and exhaust extension

Major Changes/Dates

First regular tractor, WDC 508, built April 16, 1935

The 10-degree cylinder head and chassis changes used first on trac-tor WDC 5226, December 30, 1936

The 45-degree cylinder head chassis changes used first on tractor WDC 9790, February 10, 1939

Comments

None

International I-40, IA-40, IK-40

Engine...inline, valve in head, removable sleeves
Cylinders 6
Bore and stroke...3 3/4x4 inches
Displacement ....298 cubic inches
Rated rpm 1,750
Compression ratio...na
Ignition..IH F-6 magneto
Carburetor...Zenith 50-AY-12
Cooling capacity ....12 gallons
Fuel tank capacity ....31 gallons, 1 1/4 gallons starting
Horsepower ratings.......................................na
Length...139 inches
Wheelbase...85 inches
Height ....82 inches (at steering wheel)
Width ....65 1/4 inches
Available treads ....54 inches (front), 71 inches (rear
                                                                    duals center to center)
Weight ....9,550 pounds (shipping weight)
Speed, forward, 12.75x28 rear tires

Gear	Speed
1	2 mph
2	3 5/8 mph
3	7 mph
4	11 1/8 mph
Reverse	3 mph

Price ....na
Nebraska test number....................................industrials not tested
Numbers produced...na
Serial numbers

1936	501–520
1937	521–618
1938	619–676
1939	677–770
1940	771–849

Chassis prefixes ....IAC (IA-40) or IKC (IK-40)
Engine prefixes..IAC (IA-40) or IKE (IK-40)

Chassis suffixes

H...grader tractors with differential lock
M..modified
S...special attachment
P ....pneumatic tires
T ....high-speed transmission
B ....belt pulley or PTO
W ....low-speed transmission
Engine suffixes.................................na
Chassis serial number location ....na
Engine serial number location.......................na

Regular Equipment
Magneto, pintle-hook drawbar, spring-cushion seat, hand and foot brakes, foot accelerator, muffler, air cleaner, oil filter, radiator curtain, and front pull hook

Attachments and Special Features
Lighting equipment, belt pulley, fenders, PTO, special wheel and tire equipment, tire pump, adjustable radiator shutter, etc.

Major Changes/Dates
IA-40 discontinued January 8, 1937, in favor of regular engines operating on both kerosene and gasoline
WK-40 transmission changed to accommodate increase in rpm (from 1,600 to 1,750) starting on WKC 5158, produced December 2, 1936
I-40 tractors fitted with 3 3/4x4 kerosene engines to be known as IK-40, reported effective August 27, 1936

Comments
None

International ID-40
Engine ....diesel, inline, gasoline start
Cylinders ....four
Bore and stroke ....4 3/4x6 inches
Displacement ....355 cubic inches
Rated rpm ....1,100 or 1,200
Compression ratio 17:1
Ignition..IH F-4 magneto
Carburetor...IH C-12
Cooling capacity ....14 gallons
Fuel tank capacity ....31 gallons, 1 1/4 gallons starting
Horsepower ratings..na
Length...139 inches
Wheelbase...85 inches
Height ....70 inches

Width ....641/4 inches (front), 96 inches (rear)
Available treads ....54 inches (front), 71 inches rear
(pneumatic duals, center to center)
Weight ....10,550 pounds (shipping weight)
Speed

Gear	Speed	
	1,000 rpm	1,200 rpm
1	2 1/8 mph	2 1/4 mph
2	4 mph	4 1/4 mph
3	7 mph	7 3/8 mph
4	10 3/8 mph	11 1/4 mph
Reverse	3 1/4 mph	3 mph

Price ....na
Nebraska test number..................................industrials not tested
Numbers produced.......................................na
Serial numbers ....see I-40 listing
Chassis prefixes ....IDC
Engine prefixes...WDC, WDCE, or IDCE
Chassis suffixes
H ....grader tractors with differential lock
M...modified
S ....special attachment
P ....pneumatic tires
T ....high-speed transmission
B ....belt pulley or PTO
W...low-speed transmission
Engine suffixes...na
Chassis serial number location ....na
Engine serial number location.......................na

Regular Equipment

Magneto, pintle-hook drawbar, spring-cushion seat, hand and foot brakes, foot accelerator, muffler, air cleaner, oil filter, radiator curtain, and starting equipment

Attachments and Special Features

Lighting equipment, belt pulley, fenders, PTO, special wheel and tire equipment, tire pump, etc.

Major Changes/Dates

The 10-degree cylinder head and chassis changes used first on tractor IDC 533, produced January 4, 1937

The 45-degree cylinder head chassis changes were first used on tractor IDC 693, reported February 17, 1939

Comments

None

FARMALL F-12
The Farmall F-12 was another IH innovation that caused problems for the competition. The F-12 was a smaller Farmall, perfect for small farms in the grip of the Great Depression. It featured a novel frame/transmission construction that was later carried over for the Letter Series Farmalls. *State Historical Society of Wisconsin*

Farmall F-12

Engine	Waukesha or IH inline
Cylinders	four
Bore and stroke	3x4 inches
Displacement	113 cubic inches
Rated rpm	1,400
Compression ratio	na
Ignition	IH E4a (FS 501–2048 except FS 600–608) or F-4 magneto (FS 2049–up)
Carburetor	Zenith 93 1/2W (FS 501–3034, except FS 600–608) or 1-inch IH downdraft Model A-10 (several different; FS 600–608 and FS 3035–up)
Cooling capacity	3 gallons
Fuel tank capacity	13 gallons
Horsepower ratings	na
Length	125 1/4 inches

Wheelbase..76 inches
Height ....na
Width ....74 1/4 inches
Available treads..8 inches (front, steel), 44–79 inches (rear)
Weight ....2,700 pounds
Speed
   Gear..*Speed*
   1 ....2 1/4 mph
   2 ....3 mph
   3 ....3 3/4 mph
   Reverse ....2 1/4 mph
Price ....$525 (with belt pulley, PTO, 54-inch-diameter steel wheels) or $570 (with wide front axle; 1934)
Nebraska test number....................................212 and 220
Numbers produced..na
Serial numbers
   1932...501–525
   1933...526–4880
   1934...4881–17410
   1935...17411–48659
   1936...48660–81836
   1937...81837–117517
   1938...117518–123942 (then to F-14)
Chassis prefixes ....FS
Engine prefixes...FS
Chassis serial number location ....front gas tank support
Engine serial number location.......................na

Regular Equipment

Belt pulley, PTO, air cleaner, IH magneto, adjustable rear wheel tread, and gasoline carburetor and manifold

Attachments and Special Features

Wide-tread front axles, pneumatic front and rear tires, single-rim steel rear wheels, kerosene attachment, rear wheel fenders, variety of lugs and extensions for steel wheels, electric lighting attachment, front wheel double-end mud scraper attachment, lister skid ring attachment, radiator screen and guard, single front wheel, and hydraulic lift

Major Changes/Dates

First 25 were preproduction tractors (FS 501–525); seven were built before this as well

First preproduction tractor, FS 501, was built August 17, 1932
First production tractor, FS 526, was built January 11, 1933
First tractor with IH-produced engine was FS 3032, built May 23, 1933

Tractors FS 1948–1952 have experimental Waukesha FL motors with dry sleeves

Seat-post plate 26309-D added to strengthen the transmission cover starting with FS 3282 on June 27, 1933 (retrofitted to earlier tractors)

First F-12 with kerosene attachment was FS 4656, built September 14, 1933

Revised front bolster (3519D) first used on tractor FB 11756, built June 7, 1934

First quick-attach drawbar used on tractor FS 42300, July 25, 1935

Last F-12, tractor FS-123942, built January 27, 1938

Comments

IH offered complete changeover kits to change tractors with-Waukesha engines over to IH-produced engines

Tractor replaced by Model F-14

Tractors FS 501–525 are pre-production

McCormick-Deering W-12

Engine	vertical, removable sleeves, overhead valves
Cylinders	four
Bore and stroke	3x4 inches
Displacement	113 cubic inches
Rated rpm	1,700
Compression ratio	na
Ignition	IH F-4 magneto or Robert Bosch FU4 BRS 505 special
Carburetor	1-inch IH A-10 downdraft
Cooling capacity	3 3/4 gallons
Fuel tank capacity	11 gallons
Horsepower ratings	
Drawbar	10.46 (IH)
PTO/belt	16.07 (IH)
Length	103 inches
Wheelbase	60 inches
Height	55 inches (at steering wheel)
Width	50 inches
Available treads	40 3/4 inches (front), 42 1/4 inches (rear)
Weight	2,900 pounds (shipping weight)
Speed	

Gear	Speed
1	2.14 mph
2	2.8 mph
3	3.6 mph
Reverse	2.16 mph

Price	na

Nebraska test number....................................229 and 231
Numbers produced..3,633
Serial numbers
    1934 503–1355
    1935 1356–2030
    1936 2031–2767
    1937 2768–3798
    1938 ....3799–4133 (then to W–14)
Chassis prefixes ....WS
Engine prefixes..WS
Chassis suffixes..na
Engine suffixes...na
Chassis serial number location ....plate on front fuel tank support
Engine serial number location.......................na

Regular Equipment
Magneto, air cleaner, fenders, swinging drawbar, hand brake, spring-cushion seat, PTO, and front pull hook

Attachments and Special Features
Electric lights, kerosene burning equipment, belt pulley, pneumatic tires, and adjustable drawbar hitch

Major Changes/Dates
First W-12 WS-503 built February 9, 1934

Comments
Tractor replaced by W-14

McCormick-Deering O-12
Engine...vertical, removable sleeves, overhead valves
Cylinders ....four
Bore and stroke..3x4 inches
Displacement ....113 cubic inches
Rated rpm ....1,400 or 2,000
Compression ratio..na
Ignition..IH F-4 magneto or Robert Bosch FU4 BRS 505 special
Carburetor...1-inch IH A-10 downdraft
Cooling capacity ....3 gallons
Fuel tank capacity ....11 gallons
Horsepower ratings
    Drawbar..na
    PTO/belt..18.9
Length...103 inches
Wheelbase..60 inches

Height ....52 inches (at steering wheel)
Width ....50 inches
Available treads ....39 3/8 inches (front), 40 inches (rear)
Weight ....3,200 pounds (shipping weight)
Speed
Gear...*Speed (1400 rpm; 2000 rpm)*
  1 ....2 mph; 3 mph
  2 ....4 1/4 mph; 6 mph
  3 ....7 1/4 mph; 10 3/8 mph
  Reverse ....2 mph; 3 mph
Price ....na
Nebraska test number....................................na
Numbers produced.......................................2,991
Serial numbers
  1934 512–1091
  1935 1092–1625
  1936 1626–2276
  1937 2277–3260
  1938 3261–3881
  1939 3882–4287
Chassis prefixes ....OS
Engine prefixes..OS
Chassis suffixes..na
Engine suffixes...na
Chassis serial number location ....plate on front fuel tank support
Engine serial number location.......................na

Regular Equipment
    IH magneto, air cleaner, adjustable swinging drawbar, hand brake, spring-cushion seat, rear PTO, and fenders

Attachments and Special Features
    Electric lighting equipment, belt pulley, foot brake, and adjustable side-hill hitch

Major Changes/Dates
First production O-12, OS 513, built January 29, 1934

Comments
Tractor basically similar to I-12 except brakes and drawbar

International I-12
Engine ....vertical, removable sleeves, overhead valves
Cylinders ....four
Bore and stroke ....3x4 inches
Displacement ....113 cubic inches

12 SERIES SERIAL NUMBER LOCATION
Some early tractors have the serial number plate mounted just above the steering wheel mounting, as seen here on a 12 Series wheel tractor.

Rated rpm 2,000
Compression ratio ....na
Ignition..IH F-4 magneto
Carburetor..IH Model A-10
Cooling capacity ....3 gallons
Fuel tank capacity ....11 gallons
Horsepower ratings
PTO/belt..21
Length..99 inches
Wheelbase..60 inches
Height ....52 inches
Width ....50 inches
Available treads ....39 3/8 inches (front), 40 inches (rear)
Weight ....3,200 pounds (shipping weight)
Speed
   Gear..*Speed*
   1 ....3 mph
   2 ....6 mph
   3 ....10 3/8 mph
   Reverse ....3 mph
Price ....na
Nebraska test number....................................na
Numbers produced...na
Serial numbers

1934	512–774
1935	775–974
1936	975–1524
1937	1525–2494
1938	2495–2703 (IS 2704 and after are I-14 tractors)
Chassis prefixes	IS
Engine prefixes	IS
Chassis serial number location	front fuel tank support
Engine serial number location	na

Regular Equipment

Fenders, PTO, magneto, pintle-hook drawbar, spring-cushion seat, foot brakes with parking lock, foot accelerator, muffler, air cleaner, oil filter, and radiator curtain

Attachments and Special Features

Lighting equipment, belt pulley, special wheel and tire equipment, steering brakes, tire pump, etc.

Major Changes/Dates

Information not available

Comments

None

Fairway 12

Engine	vertical, removable sleeves, overhead valves
Cylinders	four
Bore and stroke	3x4 inches
Displacement	113 cubic inches
Rated rpm	1,400 or 2,000
Compression ratio	na
Ignition	IH F-4 magneto or Robert Bosch FU4 BRS 505 special
Carburetor	1-inch IH A-10 downdraft
Cooling capacity	3 gallons
Fuel tank capacity	11 gallons
Horsepower ratings	
Drawbar	na
PTO/belt	18.9 (IH)
Length	103 inches
Wheelbase	60 inches
Height	53 inches
Width	63 1/4 inches

Available treads ....44 inches (front), 47 1/4 inches (rear)
Weight ....3,050 pounds (shipping weight)
Speed
    Gear..*Speed (1,400 rpm; 2,000 rpm)*
    1 ....2 mph; 3 mph
    2 ....4 1/4 mph; 6 mph
    3 ....7 1/4 mph; 10 3/8 mph
    Reverse ....2 mph; 3 mph
Price ....na
Nebraska test number.....................................na
Numbers produced..na
Serial numbers ....see O-12 listing
Chassis prefixes ....FOS
Engine prefixes...FOS
Chassis serial number location ....plate on front fuel tank support
Engine serial number location........................na

Regular Equipment

Steel wheels with sod-puncher lugs, oil filter, fuel pump, fuel strainer, air cleaner, adjustable swinging drawbar, foot brake with parking lock, folding seat, rear PTO, and fenders

Attachments and Special Features

Electric lighting equipment, belt pulley, pneumatic tires, steering brakes, and kerosene or distillate attachments

Major Changes/Dates

First tractor produced, FOS 686, built May 15, 1934

Comments

None

Farmall F-14

Engine ....vertical inline, removable sleeves,
                                                                overhead valves
Cylinders ....four
Bore and stroke ....3x4 inches
Displacement ....113 cubic inches
Rated rpm 1,400
Compression ratio...na
Ignition...IH F-4
Carburetor..1-inch IH Model A-10 updraft
Cooling capacity ....3 gallons
Fuel tank capacity ....13 gallons
Horsepower ratings
    Drawbar..15.36 (IH)
    PTO/belt...18.21 (IH)

FARMALL F-14
The F-14, an improved F-12, was only built for two years but shared the popular-
ty of the F-12. The breather on the right side of the engine is the easiest method
of telling the difference between the two. *State Historical Society of Wisconsin*

Length..125 1/2 inches
Wheelbase...77 inches
Height ....69 inches (at steering wheel)
Width ....74 1/4 inches (ends of axles)
Available treads ....44 1/2 to 79 inches (rear), 7 3/4
                                                                    inches (front)
Weight ....2,800 pounds
Speed
    Gear..*Speed*
    1 ....2 1/4 mph
    2 ....3 mph
    3 ....3 3/4 mph
    Reverse ....2 1/4 mph
Price ....$655 with steel wheels, $800 with
                                                                    pneumatic tires (1940)
Nebraska test number....................................297
Numbers produced...27,401
Serial numbers
    1938...124000–139606
    1939...139607–155902
Chassis prefixes ....FS
Engine prefixes..FS

Chassis serial number location ....plate on front fuel tank bracket
Engine serial number location.......................na

Regular Equipment

Belt pulley, quick-attachable drawbar, PTO, steel wheels (54x6 rear and 22 3/8x4 front), oil filter, air cleaner, IH magneto with impulse, replaceable cylinders, gasoline or gasoline-distillate carburetor as ordered, distillate included radiator shutter and heat indicator, and steering brake levers

Attachments and Special Features

Hydraulic power lift, wide-tread front axle, pneumatic wheels, wheel weights, high-speed transmissions (pneumatic-tired tractors only), adjustable radiator and heat indicator, fenders, electric starting and lighting, mud scrapers, radiator screen and guard, rubber-upholstered seat, wide-tread rear axle, clutch hold out attachment, automatic shifting drawbar, plain shifting hitch, lever-adjustable shifting hitch, exhaust pipe extension, spark arrester, special belt pulleys, and single cast front wheel

Major Changes/Dates

First F-14, FS 124000, built January 27, 1938
Changeover package for new and unsold F-12s to convert to F-14 authorized June 22, 1938, numbered FS 140000–142500

Comments

Tractors FS 155402–155902 were assigned to field changeovers of F-12s to F-14s.

McCormick-Deering W-14

Engine ....vertical, removable sleeves, over-
head valves
Cylinders ....four
Bore and stroke..3x4 inches
Displacement ....113 cubic inches
Rated rpm 1,650
Compression ratio..na
Ignition...IH F-4 magneto
Carburetor..1-inch IH A-10 downdraft
Cooling capacity ....3 gallons
Fuel tank capacity ....11 gallons
Horsepower ratings
Drawbar...13.95 (max), 10.46 (rated, 75 per-
cent of max) (IH)
PTO/belt ....18.90 (max), 16.07 (rated, 85 per-
cent of max) (IH)
Length..103 inches
Wheelbase..60 inches
Height ....na

Width ....50 inches
Available treads ....39 3/8 inches (front), 42 inches (rear)
Weight ....2,900 pounds (shipping weight)
Speed
   Gear ....*Speed*
   1 ....2 1/8 mph
   2 ....2 3/4 mph
   3 ....3 mph
   Reverse ....2 1/8 mph
Price ....$730 with steel wheels, $920 with
                                         pneumatic tires (1940)

Nebraska test number...................................na
Numbers produced......................................1,163
Serial numbers
   1938...4134–4609
   1939...4610–5296
Chassis prefixes ....WS
Engine prefixes ....WS
Chassis serial number location ....plate on front fuel tank bracket
Engine serial number location.......................na

Regular Equipment
    IH magneto, adjustable swinging drawbar, folding seat, PTO, replaceable cylinder sleeves, front drawbar, radiator shutter and heat indicator, front drawbar, and hand-operated steering brakes

Attachments and Special Features
    Pneumatic wheels, special high-speed transmission, exhaust muffler, exhaust extension, belt pulley, electric starting and lighting, variety of wheel and lug equipment, wheel weights, spark arrester, waterproof upholstered seat, and pneumatic tire pump, available in gasoline or distillate

Major Changes/Dates
    First W-14 engine, WS 4035, built January 27, 1938
    First W-14 tractor, WS 4134, built March 22, 1938
    Tractors WS 5248–5296 were unsold Fairway 14s converted with W-14 steering knuckles, brakes, transmission gears, front and rear wheels, and engine governing springs, for shipment to Australia

Comments
    None

McCormick-Deering O-14
Engine...vertical, removable sleeves, over-
                                       head valves
Cylinders ....four
Bore and stroke...3x4 inches

Displacement ....na
Rated rpm ....1,400 (engine could go to 2,000)
Compression ratio ....na
Ignition...IH F-4 magneto
Carburetor..1-inch IH A-10 downdraft
Cooling capacity ....3 gallons
Fuel tank capacity ....11 gallons
Horsepower ratings
    Drawbar..14.7 max, 11.0 (75 percent of max)
    PTO/belt ....17.3 max, 14.7 rated (85 percent of max)
Length..114 inches
Wheelbase..60 inches
Height ....48 inches (at radiator)
Width ....62 inches
Available treads ....45 1/4 inches (front), 42 5/8 inches (rear)
Weight ....3,490 pounds (shipping weight)
Speed
    Gear..*Speed (1,400 rpm; 2,000 rpm)*
    1 ....2 mph; 3 5/8 mph
    2 ....4 1/4 mph; 6 1/8 mph
    3 ....7 mph; 10 5/8 mph
    Reverse ....2 mph; 3 5/8 mph
Price $960 (1940)
Nebraska test number....................................na
Numbers produced...788
Serial numbers ....see O-12 listing
Chassis prefixes...FOS
Engine prefixes...OS (O-14) or FOS (Fairway 14)
Chassis serial number location ....plate on front fuel tank bracket
Engine serial number location........................na

Regular Equipment

Pneumatic tires, either gasoline or distillate equipment, variable-speed governor, PTO, foot-operated spring or hand-operated over-center clutch, foot-operated steering brakes, radiator shutter and heat indicator, grove fenders, and under-fender exhaust

Attachments and Special Features

Electric lighting and starting equipment, belt pulley (13 1/4- and 10 1/4-inch-diameter available), water proof upholstered seat, and spark-plug-type tire pump

Major Changes/Dates

First O-14 engine, OS 3320, produced January 27, 1938

First preproduction O-14 tractor, OS 3499, produced April 5, 1938
First regular production O-14, OS 3610, produced June 27, 1938

Comments
   None

Fairway 14

Engine..inline vertical, removable sleeves,
                                                              overhead valve
Cylinders ....four
Bore and stroke...3x4 inches
Displacement ....113 cubic inches
Rated rpm 1,400–2,000
Compression ratio..na
Ignition..IH F-4 magneto
Carburetor...1-inch IH A-10 downdraft
Cooling capacity ....3 gallons
Fuel tank capacity ....11 gallons
Horsepower ratings
   Drawbar
   PTO/belt 22
Length..105 1/2 inches
Wheelbase..60 inches
Height ....50 inches (at steering wheel)
Width ....63 1/2 inches
Available treads ....44 inches (front), 47 inches (rear)
Weight ....3,000 pounds
Speed

Gear	Speed (1,400 rpm; 2,000 rpm)
1	2 3/8 mph; 3 3/8 mph
2	4 mph; 5 3/4 mph
3	7 mph; 9 7/8 mph
Reverse	2 3/8 mph; 3 3/8 mph

Price ....na
Nebraska test number....................................na
Numbers produced..na
Serial numbers ....see O-14 listing
Chassis prefixes ....FOS
Engine prefixes...FOS
Chassis serial number location ....plate on front fuel tank support
Engine serial number location.......................na

Regular Equipment
   Steel wheels with sod-puncher lugs, IH magneto, air cleaner, swinging
drawbar, foot brake with parking lock, rear PTO, fenders, and folding seat

Attachments and Special Features
No battery lighting, belt pulley, low-pressure tires, steering brakes, distillate or kerosene attachments, radiator screen and guard, composition steering wheel, and spring-cushion seat

Major Changes/Dates
First Fairway 14, FOS 3569, built March 22, 1938

Comments
None

International I-14

Engine	inline vertical, removable sleeves, overhead valve
Cylinders	four
Bore and stroke	3x4 inches
Displacement	113 cubic inches
Rated rpm	2,000
Compression ratio	na
Ignition	IH F-4 magneto
Carburetor	IH Model A-10
Cooling capacity	3 gallons
Fuel tank capacity	11 gallons
Horsepower ratings	na
Length	99 inches
Wheelbase	60 inches
Height	52 inches (at steering wheel)
Width	na
Available treads	39 3/8 inches (front), 42 5/8 inches (rear)
Weight	3,200 pounds

Speed

Gear	Speed
1	3 mph
2	6 mph
3	10 3/8 mph
Reverse	3 mph

Price	na
Nebraska test number	na
Numbers produced	na

Serial numbers

1938	2704–3013
1939	3014–3598 (tractors IS 512–2703 were I-12s)
Chassis prefixes	IS
Engine prefixes	IS

Chassis serial number location ....plate on front fuel tank support

Engine serial number location......................NA

Regular Equipment

Fenders, PTO, magneto, pintle-hook drawbar, spring-cushion seat, foot brakes with parking lock, foot accelerator, muffler, air cleaner, oil filter, and radiator curtain

Attachments and Special Features

Lighting equipment, belt pulley, special wheel and tire equipment, steering brakes, tire pump, and other items

Major Changes/Dates

First I-14 engine, IS 2664, produced January 27, 1938

First I-14 tractor, I 2704, built March 23, 1938

Comments

Built at Chicago Tractor Works

FARMALL F-20

The F-20 was an improved power version of the Farmall Regular. The upward-mounted exhaust is the easiest way to tell the two apart. This one is shown with front-mounted corn planters, a very rare and valuable find today. The F-20 was produced in very large numbers from 1932 to 1939 and is still remembered as an excellent tractor. *State Historical Society of Wisconsin*

Farmall F-20 and F-20 Fairway

Engine ....inline vertical, removable sleeves, ball bearings
Cylinders ....four
Bore and stroke ....3 3/4x5 inches
Displacement ....220 cubic inches
Rated rpm 1,200
Compression ratio ....na
Ignition ....IH E4A magneto, others available including Bosch
Carburetor ....Zenith K-5
Cooling capacity ....7 1/4 gallons
Fuel tank capacity ....13 gallons, 7/8 gallon starting
Horsepower ratings
  Drawbar ....15.98 (IH)
  PTO/belt ....23.80 (IH)
Length ....140 inches
Wheelbase ....85 inches
Height ....78 5/8 inches (no lugs on wheels)
Width ....86 3/4 to 95 inches (standard)
Available treads ....74 3/8 inches and 83 inches (standard), 62 5/8 inches and 73 3/4 inches (narrow tread)
Weight ....3,950 pounds (shipping weight)
Speed, forward (steel wheels)

Gear	Speed
1	2 1/4 mph
2	2 3/4 mph
3	3 1/4 mph
4	3 3/4 mph
Reverse	2 3/4 mph

Price ....na
Nebraska test number ....221, 264, and 276
Numbers produced 154,398
Serial numbers

1932	501–3000
1933	3001–6381
1934	TA135000–135661
1935	6381–32715
1936	32716–68748
1937	68749–105596
1938	105597–130864
1939	130865–134699
1939	135700–148810

Chassis prefixes ....FA or TA
Engine prefixes ....FA or TA
Chassis suffixes ....na

Engine suffixes...na
Chassis serial number location ....plate on fuel tank support
Engine serial number location.......................na

Regular Equipment

Belt pulley, PTO, 40x6 or 42x12 rear wheels, combination distillate-kerosene and gasoline manifold, IH magneto, regular or narrow tread, adjustable radiator shutter, heat indicator, composition steering wheel, and foot brake attachment on rubber-tired tractors

Attachments and Special Features

Spark arrester, spark arrester extension, muffler or exhaust pipe extension, 5,000- and 8,000-foot-altitude pistons, low-speed attachment for tractors with 36-inch tires or 47-inch steel wheels, high-speed attachment for pneumatic-tired tractors, 8 1/2- and 17 5/8-inch belt pulleys for standard or 8 1/2- and 11 3/8-inch belt pulleys for narrow tread, single or double power lift, electric lighting attachment for tractors with or without oil filter and with or without IH or Dixie magneto, light spring seat for operator weighing 115 to 150 pounds, rear wheel fenders for steel-wheel tractors or 9.00x36 pneumatic tires, rubber upholstered seat, right-hand brake lever, adjustable drawbar hitch, foot brake attachment for steel-wheel tractors, quick-attachable plates and wrench, large variety of wheel-related items (wheels, lugs, overtires, road rings, and adjustable-tread overtires), increased-angularity front axle attachment for steel-wheel tractors, increased-angularity attachment for 5.50x16 rubber tires, double-end mud scrapers, wide front axle attachment for narrow-tread tractors, rear wheel weights (first, second, and third sets) for pneumatic tires, and rear wheel fenders

Major Changes/Dates

First F-20, FA 501, built January 5, 1932

The first Increased Power F-20, serial number FA 99301, built September 7, 1937 (new manifold 5262-D, different Zenith K-5 carburetor [35539-D]; engine produced 26 horsepower at flywheel at 1,200 rpm)

Comments

None

F-20 Cane and F-20 Narrow Tread (NT)

Engine ....inline vertical, removable sleeves, ball bearings
Cylinders ....four
Bore and stroke...3 3/4x5 inches
Displacement ....220 cubic inches
Rated rpm 1,200
Compression ratio..na

FARMALL F SERIES SERIAL NUMBER LOCATION
The early Farmalls have the serial number plate mounted on the toolbox, as seen on this F-20.

Ignition	see F-20 listing
Carburetor	see F-20 listing
Cooling capacity	7 1/4 gallons
Fuel tank capacity	13 gallons, 7/8 gallon starting

Horsepower ratings

Drawbar	21.30 (IH)
PTO/belt	28.00 (IH)
Length	140 1/2 inches
Wheelbase	85 inches
Height	67 1/4 inches (at steering wheel)
Width	na
Available treads	62 5/8 inches and 73 3/4 inches rear (NT), 58 1/4 inches (F-20 Cane)
Weight	na

Speed

Gear	Speed (NT; F-20 Cane)
1	2 1/4 mph; 2 1/2 mph
2	2 3/4 mph; 2 7/8 mph
3	3 1/4 mph; 3 3/8 mph
4	3 3/4 mph; 4 mph
Reverse	2 3/4 mph; 3 mph
Price	na
Nebraska test number	na
Numbers produced	na
Serial numbers	na

Chassis prefixes ....FA or TA
Engine prefixes..FA or TA
Chassis suffixes ....na
Engine suffixes...na
Chassis serial number location ....plate on fuel tank support
Engine serial number location.........................na

Regular Equipment
Information not available

Attachments and Special Features
Spark arrester, spark arrester extension, muffler or exhaust pipe extension, 5,000- and 8,000-foot-altitude pistons, low-speed attachment for tractors with 36-inch tires or 47-inch steel wheels, high-speed attachment for
pneumatic-tired tractors, 8 1/2- and 17 5/8-inch belt pulleys for standard or
8 1/2- and 11 3/8-inch belt pulleys for narrow tread, single or double power
lift, electric lighting attachment for tractors with or without oil filter and with
or without IH or Dixie magneto, light spring seat for operator weighing 115
to 150 pounds, rear wheel fenders for steel-wheel tractors or 9.00x36 pneumatic tires, rubber upholstered seat, right-hand brake lever, adjustable drawbar hitch, foot brake attachment for steel-wheel tractors, quick-attachable
plates and wrench, large variety of wheel-related items (wheels, lugs, overtires, road rings, and adjustable-tread overtires), increased-angularity front
axle attachment for steel-wheel tractors, increased-angularity attachment for
5.50x16 rubber tires, double-end mud scrapers, wide front axle attachment
for narrow-tread tractors, rear wheel weights (first, second, and third sets) for
pneumatic tires, and rear wheel fenders

Major Changes/Dates
F-20 Cane approved August 12, 1938
Low-speed attachment for F-20 Cane (same as for regular and narrow tread) first applied to tractor FA129651, built June 30, 1938, and
shipped to Australia July 15, 1938

Comments
F-20 Cane was based on F-20 NT, and was primarily intended for
the export trade to Australia. The F-20 Cane tractor had a wide-tread-
type front bolster, cane-type high-arch front axle, 42.00-4 angle-rim steel
rear wheels (could be fitted with pneumatic tires), 34.00x6 spoke-type
front wheels with high skid ring, and foot brakes.

McCormick-Deering W-30, W-30 Orchard, and W-30 California Orchard

Engine ....vertical inline, removable sleeves
Cylinders ....four
Bore and stroke ....4 1/4x5 inches
Displacement ....284 cubic inches

Rated rpm 1,150
Compression ratio ....na
Ignition..IH E4A, several others available, including Bosch
Carburetor...Zenith K-5
Cooling capacity ....11 gallons
Fuel tank capacity ....24 gallons, 1 gallon starting
Horsepower ratings
    Drawbar..19.7 (IH)
    PTO/belt ....31.3 (IH)
Length...120 3/4 inches
Wheelbase...72 inches
Height ....62 3/4 inches
Width ....66 1/4 inches
Available treads ....45 inches (front), 53 1/4 inches (rear)
Weight ....4,820 pounds (shipping weight)
Speed

Gear	Speed
1	2 mph
2	3 1/4 mph
3	3 3/4 mph
Reverse	2 3/4 mph

Price ....$975 with belt pulley (1934), $987 with orchard equipment (low seat, orchard fenders, and apron)
Nebraska test number......................................210
Numbers produced..na
Serial numbers
    1932..501–521
    1933..522–547
    1934..548–3181
    1935..3182–9722
    1936..9723–15094
    1937..15095–23833
    1938..23834–29921
    1939..29922–32481
    1940..32482–33041
Chassis prefixes ....WB
Engine prefixes...XC
Chassis suffixes
    S ....special features
    P ....pneumatic tires
    M..modified
    SP..four-speed transmission(15 mph; on tractors below WB 15106)
    T ....four-speed transmission (10 mph; tractors WB 15106 and up)

HA...high-altitude pistons
SL...lower low gear
H...differential lock
Engine suffixes
D...distillate
Chassis serial number location ....plate on rear fuel tank support
Engine serial number location.......................na

Regular Equipment

IH magneto, belt pulley, variable-speed governor, radiator shutter and heat indicator, manifold heat control valve, replaceable cylinder sleeves, adjustable drawbar, external-contracting brake with hand lever and foot ratchet, and front drawbar

Attachments and Special Features

PTO, lighting equipment, special wheel and lug equipment, pneumatic tires, special belt pulleys, sliding drawbar, spark arrester, four-speed transmission, low seat and controls for orchards and groves, orchard fenders and platform, waterproof upholstered seat cushion, exhaust extension pipe, exhaust muffler, and tire pump

Major Changes/Dates

First I-30 tractor, IB-512, produced May 24, 1932
New fender 21068DA (right) displaced 21068D, and 21069DA (left) replaced 21069D starting on tractor WB 24915 to improve bead; produced October 26, 1938

Comments

Tractors shipped to Jacksonville, Florida, had I-30 four-speed transmissions

International I-30

Engine ....vertical inline, removable sleeves
Cylinders ....four
Bore and stroke...4 1/4x5 inches
Displacement ....284 cubic inches
Rated rpm 1,150
Compression ratio...na
Ignition...IH E4A magneto
Carburetor..Zenith
Cooling capacity ....11 gallons
Fuel tank capacity ....23 gallons
Horsepower ratings
PTO/ belt 35
Length..121 inches
Wheelbase..78 inches
Height ....62 3/8 inches

Width ....65 1/4 inches
Available treads ....52 inches (front), 63 inches (rear;
                         dual pneumatic)
Weight ....7,550 pounds (shipping weight)
Speed

Gear	Speed
1	2 mph
2	4 mph
3	7 1/4 mph
4	12 1/4 mph
Reverse	3 mph

Price ....na
Nebraska test number...................................industrials not tested
Numbers produced..na
Serial numbers

1931	501–513
1932	514–665
1933	666–874
1934	875–1329
1935	1330–2075
1936	2076–3383
1937	3384–4595
1938	4596–4983
1939	4984–5323
1940	5323–5468

Chassis prefixes ....IB
Engine prefixes..AD
Chassis suffixes

M	modified
B	belt pulley or PTO
R	with full reverse transmission
RB	with full reverse transmission and belt pulley or PTO
RP	full reverse transmission, meaning of P unknown
D	dump body with high transmission case
DL	dump body with low transmission case (Hughs-Keenan)
DLT	dump body with low transmission case and high-speed attachment
S	special attachment
H	grader tractors with differential lock
L	lower-low transmission
HA	high-altitude pistons
X3	steel-wheel industrial No. 3

Engine suffixes..na

Chassis serial number location .... na
Engine serial number location .... na

Regular Equipment

Magneto, pintle-hook drawbar, spring-cushion seat, hand and foot brakes, foot accelerator, muffler, air cleaner, oil filter, and radiator curtain

Attachments and Special Features

Lighting equipment, belt pulley, fenders, PTO, special wheel and tire equipment, tire pump, and others

Major Changes/Dates

First I-30 tractor, IB-512, produced May 22, 1932

Comments

None

Farmall F-30

Engine	vertical inline, removable sleeves
Cylinders	four
Bore and stroke	4 1/4x5 inches
Displacement	284 cubic inches
Rated rpm	1,150
Ignition	IH E4A magneto (AA 501–7038) or IH F-4 magneto (AA 7039–up)
Carburetor	Wheeler Schebler TDFX-8 (FB 501–1128) 1 1/4-inch Zenith K5 (FB 1129–up)?
Cooling capacity	9 gallons
Fuel tank capacity	21 gallons, 1 gallon starting

Horsepower ratings

Drawbar	20.27
PTO/belt	30.29
Length	147 inches
Wheelbase	94 inches
Height	81 inches (no lugs on wheels)
Width	89 1/4 inches or 97 inches (rears in or out)
Available treads	8 inches or 11 5/8 inches (front), 77 inches or 85 inches rear (standard)
Weight	5,300 pounds (shipping weight)

Speed, forward (standard)

Gear	Speed
1	2 mph
2	2 3/4 mph
3	3 1/4 mph
4	3 3/4 mph

FARMALL F-30

At about 30 percent larger than its little brother the F-20, the F-30 was the first Farmall to be a different size than the original Regular. The F-30s, however, were not produced in nearly the numbers of their smaller siblings. *State Historical Society of Wisconsin*

Reverse	2 mph
Price	$1,025 with belt pulley, PTO, and 42-inch steel wheels (1934)
Nebraska test number	198
Numbers produced	na
Serial numbers	
1931	501–1183
1932	1184–4304
1933	4305–5525
1934	5526–7031
1935	7032–10406
1936	10407–18683
1937	18684–26848
1938	27186–28719
1939	29007–30026
Chassis prefixes	FB
Engine prefixes	AA
Chassis suffixes	
N	narrow-tread tractor
NW	narrow-tread tractor with wide front axle

CNW...narrow-tread cane tractor with wide
front axle
S ....modified tractor
W...regular tractor with wide front axle
Engine suffixes..na
Chassis serial number location ....nameplate on tool box under fuel tank
Engine serial number location......................pad on left side of engine

Regular Equipment

Belt pulley, PTO, 42.00x12 solid-rim wheels, combination kerosene-distillate and gasoline manifold, adjustable radiator shutter and heat indicator, IH magneto, composition steering wheel, regular or narrow tread, and foot brake on rubber-tired tractors

Attachments and Special Features

Wide variety of wheel, lug, road rings, overtires, extension rims, and double-end wheel scrapers for front wheels; wide-tread front axle attachment for narrow-tread tractor; two-tread front wheels for rubber-tired tractors for lister territory; increased-angularity front wheels for 6.00x16 rubber tires for wide front, single, or double power lifts; rubber upholstered seat; rear wheel fenders; electric lighting attachments; foot brake attachments for steel-wheel tractors; right-hand brake attachment; rear wheel weights for pneumatic tractors; variety of belt pulleys; and quick-attachable plates and wrench

Major Changes/Dates

First F-30 built, FB 501 (engine AA 503, transmission # 539), July 27, 1931

First engine (AA 501) assembled at Tractor Works July 15, 1931

Increased-strength front bolster (2279-DA replacing 2279-D) first used on FB 4581, built February 8, 1933, placed on earlier-built tractors starting with FB 3099, shipped June 28, 1934, to Memphis Territory

First narrow tread (FB 3286 N) built in 1932

Change from gray tractors on November 1, 1936, probably starting with tractor FB 18684

Comments

Some may have been built after 1939 to meet demand for cane tractors.

F-30 Cane, F-30 Cane Regular (1938), F-30 H.S. (1938), F-30 NT, and F-30 Rice Special

Engine ....inline, ball-bearing crankshaft
Cylinders ....four
Bore and stroke..4 1/4x5 inches
Displacement ....284 cubic inches
Rated rpm 1,150

Compression ratio...na
Ignition...IH F-4 magneto
Carburetor...Zenith K-5
Cooling capacity ....10 gallons
Fuel tank capacity ....21 gallons, 1 gallon starting
Horsepower ratings...na
Length...na
Wheelbase...na
Height ....na
Width ....na
Available treads ....72 inches front and back (1938 Regular Cane)
Weight ....na
Speed
  1935 F-30 Cane with 42-inch rear wheels

Gear	Speed
1	3.2 mph
2	4.2 mph
3	5.0 mph
4	na
Reverse	3.81 mph

  1935 F-30 Cane with 66-inch rear wheels

Gear	Speed
1	2 mph
2	2.7 mph
3	3.2 mph
4	6.8 mph
Reverse	2.4 mph

  1938 High-Speed Cane

Gear	Speed
1	3 1/8 mph
2	4 1/8 mph
3	5 mph
4	10 1/2 mph
Reverse	3 4/5 mph

  1938 High-Speed Cane with overdrive

Gear	Speed
1	5 mph
2	6 5/8 mph
3	7 7/8 mph
4	16 3/4 mph
Reverse	6 mph

  1938 Regular Cane

Gear	Speed
1	3 1/8 mph
2	4 1/8 mph
3	5 mph

```
4 ............................................10 mph
Reverse ...................................3 3/4 mph
Price ...........................................$1,060 (1934 F-30 NT with wide-
                                              tread front end)
```

```
Nebraska test number...................na
Numbers produced.......................na
Serial numbers ............................na
Chassis prefixes ..........................FB
Engine prefixes...........................AA
Chassis suffixes...........................na
Engine suffixes............................na
Chassis serial number location .......na
Engine serial number location.......na
```

Regular Equipment
   Information not available

Attachments and Special Features
   Information not available

Major Changes/Dates
   First F-30 NT (FB 3846N) built January 25, 1932
   First F-30 NT with wide front axle (FB 3747 NW) built March 4, 1932
   First Cane tractors (FB 7262–7267 CNW) shipped to New Orleans January 1935
   First F-30 High-Speed Cane tractor (1938 Model) FB 28354 built September 8, 1938
   First F-30 Regular Cane (1938 Model) FB 29006 built December 29,1938
   The 72-inch-tread front axle replaced by 66-inch-tread rear axle for both 1938 Cane tractors, first built February 17, 1939, on High-Speed Cane tractor FB 29528

Comments
   "F-30 High-Speed Cane Tractor—1938 Model" had an auxiliary transmission inserted ahead of the regular transmission, giving a 1.6:1 overdrive. The tractor had longer frame rails and controls, foot brakes, high-clearance nonadjustable front axle, cast disc-type front wheels with 5.25x21 pneumatic tires, spoke-type single-rim rear wheels with 10.00x40 cane-field pneumatic tires, and 72-inch tread front and rear
   "F-30 Regular Cane—1938 Model" was similar to earlier F-30 Cane, with these differences: high-clearance nonadjustable front axle, cast disc front wheels with 5.25x21 pneumatic tires, and spoke-type single-rim rear wheels with 10.00x40 cane-field pneumatic tires

Most of the As and Bs have the serial number plate located on the left seat support, as seen here. The Super A, the 100, and the 130 are in the same location. A few early tractors, have them mounted on the front edge of the operator's platform.

Farmall A

Engine	C-113
Cylinders	four
Bore and stroke	3x4 inches
Displacement	113.1 cubic inches
Rated rpm	1,400
Compression ratio	5.33:1 (gasoline)
Ignition	IH H-4 magneto
Carburetor	Zenith Model 161-7, Marvel Schebler TSX-156 (kerosene or distillate), or Marvel Schebler TSX-157 (gasoline)
Cooling capacity	3 1/4 gallons
Fuel tank capacity	10 gallons, 1 gallon starting

Horsepower ratings

Drawbar	15.53 distillate, 17.35 gasoline
PTO/belt	19.06 gasoline, 17.12 distillate
Length	106 1/4 inches
Wheelbase	71 1/8 inches
Height	63 1/4 inches steering wheel
Width	76 3/4 inches rear wheels, 55 7/8 inches rear axles
Available treads	40–68 inches (adjustable rear), 43 inches (fixed front), or 44–64 inches (adjustable front)
Weight	1,870 pounds

Speed

Gear	Speed
1	2 1/4 mph
2	3 mph
3	4 5/8 mph
4	9 5/8 mph
Reverse	2 3/4 mph
Price	$515 (1940) with vertically adjustable drawbar, upholstered seat, fenders, nonadjustable front axle, but without PTO or pulley

Nebraska test number....................................329 and 330
Numbers produced (includes AV, International A)
   1939...na
   1940...22,023
   1941...22,950
   1942...9,579
   1943...105
   1944...8,177
   1945...18,494
   1946...19,739
   1947...20,937 (includes some Super As)
   1948...15,869 (includes Super A)
   117,552 Farmall As produced
Serial numbers (includes AV, B, BN)
   1939...501–6743
   1940...6744–41499
   1941...41500–80738
   1942...80739–96389
   1943...officially, no production
   1944...96390–113217
   1945...113218–146699
   1946...146700–182963
   1947...182964–198298 (Chicago)
   1947...200001–220829 (Louisville)
   1948...na
Chassis prefixes ....FAA
Engine prefixes...FAA
Chassis serial number location ....left seat support bracket
Engine serial number location......................upper right side of engine

Regular Equipment
   IH magneto, 8.00x24 pneumatic rear tires, 4.00x15 front tires, and rear fenders

Attachments and Special Features
   Belt pulley and PTO attachment, PTO-only attachment, 5,000- and 8,000-foot high-altitude pistons, kerosene-distillate attachment including adjustable radiator shutter and heat indicator, adjustable radiator shutter and heat indicator for gasoline tractors, muffler, lighting attachment including generator and battery, swinging drawbar, adjustable front axle, wheel weights, and a variety of wheel and tire equipment

Major Changes/Dates
   First A (FAA 501) built June 21, 1939
   Tractors FAA 28577–29450 built with different gear material for trial
   Oil filter changed from star type (tall casing) to umbrella type (short casing) starting on FAA 97938, built May 16, 1944

Comments

   Tractors from 501–201000 have matching engine and chassis serial numbers

Farmall AV

Engine C-113
Cylinders .... four
Bore and stroke .... 3x4 inches
Displacement .... 113 cubic inches
Rated rpm 1,400
Compression ratio .... 5.33:1 (gasoline)
Ignition .... IH H-4 magneto
Carburetor .... Zenith Model 161-7, Marvel Schebler TSX-156 (kerosene or distillate), or Marvel Schebler TSX-157 (gasoline)
Cooling capacity .... 3 1/4 gallons
Fuel tank capacity .... 10 gallons, 1 gallon starting
Horsepower ratings
   Drawbar 17
   PTO/belt 19
Length .... 115 3/8 inches
Wheelbase .... 71 3/4 inches
Height .... 69 1/4 inches (at steering wheel)
Width .... 76 3/8 inches (rear wheels), 60 5/8 inches (rear axles)
Available treads .... 44–68 inches (front), 48–68 inches (rear 4-inch spaces)
Weight .... 2,280 pounds
Speed, forward, 8-36 tires

Gear	Speed
1	2 7/8 mph
2	4 5/8 mph
3	6 1/8 mph
4	12 3/4 mph
Reverse	3 5/8 mph

Price .... na
Nebraska test number .... na
Numbers produced 3,603
Serial numbers .... see Farmall A listing
Chassis prefixes .... FAAV
Engine prefixes .... FAAV
Chassis serial number location .... left seat support bracket
Engine serial number location .... upper right side of engine

Regular Equipment
   Information not available

Attachments and Special Features

Belt pulley, belt pulley and PTO, PTO, muffler, distillate-burning equipment, electric starting and lighting, spark arrester, double-groove fan and generator pulley, tire pumps, 5,000- and 8,000-foot pistons, and wheel weights

Major Changes/Dates

First AV (FAAV 48562) built January 10, 1941

Oil filter changed from star type (tall casing) to umbrella type (short casing) on FAA 97938, built May 16, 1944

Comments

Tractors from 501–201000 have matching engine and chassis serial numbers

International A

Engine	C-113
Cylinders	four
Bore and stroke	3x4 inches
Displacement	113 cubic inches
Rated rpm	1,400
Compression ratio	5.33:1 (gasoline)
Ignition	IH H-4 magneto
Carburetor	Zenith Model 161-7, Marvel Schebler TSX-156 (kerosene or distillate), or Marvel Schebler TSX-157 (gasoline)
Cooling capacity	3 3/8 gallons
Fuel tank capacity	10 gallons
Horsepower ratings	
Drawbar	17.35 (IH)
PTO/belt	na
Length	105 inches
Wheelbase	70 inches
Height	na
Width	69 inches with mower bar up
Available treads	60 inches
Weight	2,750 pounds

Speed

Gear	Speed
1	2 1/4 mph
2	3 mph
3	4 5/8 mph
4	9 5/8 mph
Reverse	2 3/4 mph

Price	na
Nebraska test number	na
Numbers produced	na
Serial numbers	see Farmall A listing

Chassis prefixes 1AA
Engine prefixes...IAA
Chassis serial number location ....left seat support bracket
Engine serial number location.......................upper right side of engine

Regular Equipment
Information not available

Attachments and Special Features
Information not available

Major Changes/Dates
Information not available

Comments
Industrial version of Farmall A, distinguishable by heavy-duty square front axle, decals, International nameplate on radiator, and foot-operated governor control

Chassis and engine prefixes are often referred to as either "1AA" or "IAA" in IH references—and sometimes both in the same reference book. Prefix "1AA" is more frequently seen on tractors

Tractors from 501–201000 have matching engine and chassis serial numbers

Farmall Super A
Engine C-113
Cylinders ....four
Bore and stroke..3x4 inches
Displacement ....113 cubic inches
Rated rpm 1,400
Compression ratio..6.0:1
Ignition..6-volt battery
Carburetor...Carter, Marvel Schebler TSX-157 (gasoline), or TSX-156 (distillate or kerosene); or Zenith 167x7 or 67x7

FARMALL SUPER A
This Farmall Super A is fitted with a belly blade, a very desirable implement today. This Super A model's decal is the early version with the "Super" on a curved line through the "A." *State Historical Society of Wisconsin*

Cooling capacity ....3 1/4 gallons
Fuel tank capacity ....11 gallons
Horsepower ratings
    Drawbar..17.35 (IH)
    PTO/belt ....19.06 (IH)
Length...106 7/8 inches
Wheelbase...71 1/8 inches
Height ....64 1/4 inches (at steering wheel)
Width ....78 inches rear wheels set out, 55
    7/8 to ends of rear axles
Available treads ....40–68 inches (rear), 44–64
    inches (front)
Weight ....2,385 pounds
Speed
    Gear..*Speed*
    1 ....2 3/8 mph
    2 ....3 5/8 mph
    3 ....4 7/8 mph
    4 ....10 mph
    Reverse ....2 7/8 mph
Price $1,150 (1954)
Nebraska test number....................................na
Numbers produced (includes AV, International A)
    1947 ....na
    1948 15,869
    1949 13,805
    1950 16,376
    1951 27,562
    1952 11,334
    1953 17,909
    1954 5,953
    94,001 Farmall Super As produced
Serial numbers
    1947 250001–250081
    1948 250082–268195
    1949 268196–281268
    1950 281269–300125
    1951 300126–324469
    1952 324470–336879
    1953 336880–353347
    1954 353348–357958
Chassis prefixes ....FAA
Engine prefixes...FAAM
Chassis serial number location ....plate on right side of tool box and
    seat support
Engine serial number location.......................pad on upper right side of
    crankcase

Regular Equipment

Four-speed transmission, gasoline or distillate (included radiator shutter) engine, IH magneto, upholstered seat, foot brakes, fenders, quick-change vertically adjustable drawbar, nonadjustable front axle, and pneumatic tires

Attachments and Special Features

Distillate engine, magneto ignition, air pipe extension, collector pre-cleaner, dual rear lamp, pre-screener, spark arrester, wheel weights, jute-upholstered seat, high-altitude pistons, radiator shutter with heat indicator, seed-plate drive, remote control, exhaust valve rotators, Touch Control, adjustable front axle, and a variety of wheel and tire equipment

Major Changes/Dates

Information not available

Comments

Early 1950 models painted white

Farmall Super AV

Engine	C-113
Cylinders	four
Bore and stroke	3x4 inches
Displacement	113 cubic inches
Rated rpm	1,400
Compression ratio	6.0:1
Ignition	6-volt battery
Carburetor	Carter, Marvel Schebler TSX-157 (gasoline), or TSX-156 (distillate or kerosene); or Zenith 167x7 or 67x7
Cooling capacity	3 1/4 gallons
Fuel tank capacity	11 gallons
Horsepower ratings	
Drawbar	19
PTO/belt	17
Length	115 inches
Wheelbase	71 5/8 inches
Height	70 inches (at steering wheel)
Width	77 3/4 inches (wheels set out), 60 5/8 inches (rear axles)
Available treads	48–68 inches (rear), 44–68 inches (front)
Weight	2,825 pounds
Speed	

Gear	Speed
1	3 mph
2	4 7/8 mph
3	6 3/8 mph

4	13 1/4 mph
Reverse	3 3/4 mph
Price	$1,509 (in 1954)
Nebraska test number	na
Numbers produced	na
Serial numbers	see Farmall Super A listing
Chassis prefixes	FAAV
Engine prefixes	FAAVM
Chassis serial number location	plate on right side of tool box and seat support
Engine serial number location	pad on upper right side of crankcase

Regular Equipment

Gasoline or distillate engine (distillate included radiator shutter), IH ignition, upholstered seat, foot-operated differential brakes, fenders, quick-change vertically adjustable drawbar, adjustable front axle, 4.00x19 front tires, and 8.00x36 or 9.00x36 rear tires

Attachments and Special Features

Distillate engine, magneto ignition, air pipe extension, collector pre-cleaner, pre-screener, dual rear lamp, spark arrester, wheel weights, jute-upholstered seat, high-altitude pistons, radiator shutter with heat indicator, remote-control hydraulics, exhaust valve rotators, seed-plate drive, swinging drawbar, muffler, Touch Control, wheel weights, and pneumatic tire pump

Major Changes/Dates

Information not available

Comments

Early 1950 models painted white

INTERNATIONAL SUPER A

Here is an International Super A doing its intended duty—roadside mowing. Notice the white model decal with the "Super" over the "A." *State Historical Society of Wisconsin*

International Super A

Engine	valve in head, replaceable sleeves
Cylinders	four
Bore and stroke	3x4 inches
Displacement	113.1 cubic inches

Rated rpm 1,400
Compression ratio..6.0:1
Ignition..IH H-4
Carburetor..Carter or Zenith 161x7 250001-255417,
Zenith 67x7 255418 and up,
Marvel Schebler TSX-157 250001-255417 (gasoline),
Marvel Schebler TSX-157 TSX-156 250001-255417 (kerosene distillate)
Cooling capacity ....3 1/4 gallons or more
Fuel tank capacity ....11 gallons
Horsepower ratings
    Drawbar..17.35 (IH)
    PTO/belt ....19.06 (IH)
Length..106 inches
Wheelbase..71 1/4 inches
Height..81 7/8 inches (at top of muffler)
Width ....68 3/4 inches
Available treads ....44–64 inches (front), 40–68 inches (rear)
Weight ....2,680 pounds with AI-23 highway mower

Speed

Gear	Speeds
1	2.1 mph
2	3.4 mph
3	4.5 mph
4	9.3 mph
Reverse	2.7 mph

Price ....na
Nebraska test number....................................na
Numbers produced...838
Serial numbers ....see Farmall Super A listing
Chassis prefixes ....IAA
Engine prefixes..IAAM
Chassis serial number location ....plate on right side of tool box and seat support
Engine serial number location........................pad on upper right side of crankcase

Regular Equipment
    Information not available

Attachments and Special Features
    Electric lighting and starting, radiator shutter with heat indicator, exhaust muffler, spark arrester, belt pulley, front and rear wheel weights,

distillate fuel equipment, rack for extra knives, and power-drive knife grinder (requires belt pulley)

Major Changes/Dates
Information not available

Comments
None

Farmall Super A-1

Engine	C-123
Cylinders	four
Bore and stroke	3 1/8x4 inches
Displacement	123 cubic inches
Rated rpm	1,450
Compression ratio	6.01:1
Ignition	6-volt battery
Carburetor	Carter or Zenith 67x7
Cooling capacity	15 quarts
Fuel tank capacity	11 gallons
Horsepower ratings	na
Length	106 7/8 inches
Wheelbase	71 1/8 inches
Height	64 1/4 inches (at top of steering wheel), 81 3/4 inches (at top of muffler)
Width	55 7/8 inches minimum, 78 inches maximum
Available treads	43 inches nonadjustable or 44–64 inches adjustable front (4-inch intervals), 40–68 inches rear (4-inch intervals)
Weight	na

Speed

Gear	Speed
1	2 3/8 mph
2	3 5/8 mph
3	4 7/8 mph
4	10 mph
Reverse	2 7/8 mph

Price	na
Nebraska test number	na
Numbers produced	1,672

Serial numbers

1954	356001–357958
Chassis prefixes	FAA-1
Engine prefixes	FCM

Chassis serial number location............................right side of tool box and seat suppor
Engine serial number location.......................upper right side of engine crankcase

Regular Equipment
Information not available

Attachments and Special Features
Adjustable wide-tread front axle, air pipe extension, belt pulley and PTO, belt pulley, combination rear light and taillight, detachable sea pad, deluxe detachable seat pad, deluxe upholstered seat, engine hou meter, exhaust meter, exhaust valve rotators, wheel weights, hydrauli remote control, pneumatic tire pump (Schrader and Engineair), PTO pre-cleaner (collector and detachable sleeve types), pre-screener, radia tor shutter, seed-plate drive, spark arrester, 5,000- and 8,000-foot high altitude pistons (gasoline or distillate), and 5,000- or 8,000-foot high-alti tude pistons (kerosene)

Major Changes/Dates
Information not available

Comments
No attempt was made by the factory to match engine and tracto serial numbers

Farmall Super AV-1

Engine...C-123
Cylinders ....four
Bore and stroke...3 1/8x4 inches
Displacement ....123 cubic inches
Rated rpm 1,450
Compression ratio...na
Ignition..6-volt battery
Carburetor..Carter or Zenith 67x7
Cooling capacity ....15 quarts
Fuel tank capacity ....11 gallons
Horsepower ratings...na
Length...115 inches
Wheelbase..71 5/8 inches
Height ....70 inches (at top of steering wheel), 88 inches (at top of muffler)
Width ....60 5/8 inches minimum, 77 3/4 inches maximum
Available treads ....44–68 inches front (4-inch intervals), 48–68 inches rear (4-inch intervals)
Weight ....2,762 pounds
Speed, forward, 9-36 tires

Gear..*Speed*
1 ....3 mph
2 ....4 7/8 mph
3 ....6 3/8 mph
4 ....13 1/4 mph
Reverse ....3 3/4 mph
Price ....na
Nebraska test number...................................na
Numbers produced.......................................228
Serial numbers ....see Farmall Super A-1 listing
Chassis prefixes FAAV-1
Engine prefixes..FCM
Chassis serial number location ....right side of tool box and seat sup-
                                                                            port
Engine serial number location......................upper right side of engine crankcase

Regular Equipment
    Information not available

Attachments and Special Features
    Air pipe extension, belt pulley and PTO, belt pulley, combination rear light and taillight, detachable seat pad, deluxe detachable seat pad, deluxe upholstered seat, engine hour meter, exhaust meter, exhaust valve rotators, wheel weights, hydraulic remote control, pneumatic tire pump (Schrader and Engineair), PTO, pre-cleaner (collector and detachable sleeve types), pre-screener, radiator shutter, seed-plate drive, spark arrester, 5,000- and 8,000-foot high-altitude pistons (gasoline or distillate), and 5,000- or 8,000-foot high-altitude pistons (kerosene)

Major Changes/Dates
    Information not available

Comments
    No attempt was made by the factory to match engine and tractor serial numbers

International Super A-1

Engine C-123
Cylinders ....four
Bore and stroke...3 1/8x4 inches
Displacement ....123 cubic inches
Rated rpm 1,450
Compression ratio...na
Ignition...6-volt battery
Carburetor...Zenith 67x7 or Carter
Cooling capacity ....15 quarts
Fuel tank capacity ....11 gallons

Horsepower ratings ....na
Length ....na
Wheelbase ....na
Height ....na
Width ....na
Available treads ....na
Weight ....na
Speed ....na
Price ....na
Nebraska test number ....na
Numbers produced ....na
Serial numbers ....see Farmall Super A-1 listing
Chassis prefixes IAA-1
Engine prefixes ....ICM
Chassis serial number location ....plate on right side of tool box
under seat
Engine serial number location ....stamped on upper right side of engine

Regular Equipment
Information not available

Attachments and Special Features
Information not available

Major Changes/Dates
Information not available

Comments
No attempt was made by the factory to match engine and tractor serial numbers.

Farmall B

Engine C-113
Cylinders ....four
Bore and stroke ....3x4 inches
Displacement ....113.1 cubic inches
Rated rpm 1,400
Compression ratio ....5.33:1 (gasoline)
Ignition ....IH H-4 magneto
Carburetor ....Zenith Model 161-7, Marvel Schebler TSX-156 (kerosene or distillate), or TSX-157 (gasoline)
Cooling capacity ....3 1/4 gallons
Fuel tank capacity ....10 gallons, 1 gallon starting
Horsepower ratings
Drawbar ....17.31 gasoline, 15.29 distillate
PTO/belt ....19.22 gasoline, 16.70 distillate

FARMALL B
The Farmall B was the two-row equivalent of the Farmall A, with tricycle front wheels and a long left axle; it would eventually be replaced by the Farmall C. A McCormick-Deering No. 42 combine can be seen at work behind the B. *State Historical Society of Wisconsin*

Length	107 7/8 inches
Wheelbase	72 3/4 inches
Height	65 inches
Width	100 1/2 inches (rear wheels), 79 1/4 inches (rear axles)
Available treads	64–92 inches (rear)
Weight	1,830 pounds

Speed

Gear	Speed
1	2 1/4 mph
2	3 mph
3	4 5/8 mph
4	9 5/8 mph
Reverse	2 3/4 mph

Price	$535 (1940)
Nebraska test number	331 and 332

Numbers produced (includes BN)

1940	12,765
1941	16,553
1942	6,305
1943	5
1944	7,933
1945	12,951
1946	14,623
1947	20,100
1948	1,921

75,241 Farmall Bs produced

Serial numbers	see Farmall A listing
Chassis prefixes	FAB

Engine prefixes...FAB
Chassis serial number location ....left seat support bracket
Engine serial number location........................upper right side of engine

Regular Equipment

IH magneto, 8.00x24 pneumatic rear tires, 6.00x12 front tire, and rear fenders

Attachments and Special Features

Belt pulley and PTO attachment, PTO attachment only, belt pulley only, 5,000- and 8,000-foot high-altitude pistons, kerosene-distillate attachment including adjustable radiator shutter and heat indicator, adjustable radiator shutter and heat indicator for gasoline tractors, muffler, lighting attachment (including generator, battery, and other parts), swinging drawbar, and a variety of wheel and tire equipment

Major Changes/Dates

First B (FAB 3675) built September 5, 1939
Tractors FAB 18247–18322 built with different material gears
Oil filter changed from star type (tall casing) to umbrella type (short casing) starting on FAA 97938, built May 16, 1944

Comments

Tractors from 501–201000 have matching engine and chassis serial numbers

Farmall BN

Engine C-113
Cylinders ....four
Bore and stroke..3x4 inches
Displacement ....113.1 cubic inches
Rated rpm 1,400
Compression ratio..5.33:1 (gasoline)
Ignition..IH H-4 magneto
Carburetor..Zenith Model 161-7, Marvel Schebler
TSX-156 (kerosene or distillate), or
Marvel Schebler TSX-157 (gasoline)
Cooling capacity ....3 1/4 gallons
Fuel tank capacity ....10 gallons, 1 gallon starting
Horsepower ratings
    Drawbar...17
    PTO/belt 19
Length...107 7/8 inches
Wheelbase..72 3/4 inches
Height ....65 inches (at top of steering wheel)
Width ....92 1/2 inches (wheels), 71 1/4 inches (axles)

Available treads ....56–84 inches (rear)
Weight ....1,780 pounds
Speed

Gear	Speed
1	2 1/4 mph
2	3 mph
3	4 5/8 mph
4	9 5/8 mph
Reverse	2 3/4 mph

Price ....na
Nebraska test number.....................................na
Numbers produced...14,967
Serial numbers ....see Farmall A listing
Chassis prefixes ....see comments
Engine prefixes..see comments
Chassis serial number location ....left seat support bracket
Engine serial number location.......................upper right side of engine

Regular Equipment
Same as Farmall B

Attachments and Special Features
Same as Farmall B

Major Changes/Dates
First BN (FAB 39715X7) built October 31, 1940

Oil filter changed from star type (tall casing) to umbrella type (short casing) starting on FAA 97938, built May 16, 1944

Comments
Tractors from 501–201000 have matching engine and chassis serial numbers

Model BNs from 39715–48350 have serial prefix "FAA" and suffix X-7. After 48350, tractors have FABN prefix

Farmall H

Engine ....C-152 vertical inline, removable sleeves, overhead valves
Cylinders ....four
Bore and stroke ....3 3/8x4 1/4 inches
Displacement ....152.1 cubic inches
Rated rpm 1,650
Compression ratio..5.9:1
Ignition..IH H-4 magneto
Carburetor..1-inch IH D-10 updraft
Cooling capacity ....4 1/4 gallons
Fuel tank capacity ....17 gallons, 1 gallon starting tank

FARMALL H

The Farmall H was in its early years the best selling IH tractor; although by the late 1940s, it was surpassed by the M. The H, the middle range Farmall, was enormously popular, being very similar in appearance to the M, with minor differences noticeable in the transmission casing. *State Historical Society of Wisconsin*

Horsepower ratings
Drawbar	22.65 distillate, 25.5 gasoline (IH)
PTO/belt	24.34 distillate, 27.9 gasoline (IH)
Length	125 1/4 inches
Wheelbase	88 1/2 inches
Height	74 inches (at top of steering wheel)
Width	90 3/4 inches (rear wheels), 75 inches (rear axles)
Available treads	44–80 inches (rear), 8 1/8 inches (front)
Weight equipped	3,725 pounds

Speed, forward, 51-inch steel wheels
Gear	Speed
1	2 5/8 mph
2	3 mph
3	4 1/4 mph
4	5 3/8 mph
5	15 5/8 mph (10-38 pneumatic tires)
Reverse	3 mph

Price	$695 with steel wheels, quick-attachable drawbar, but without PTO or pulley (1940); $855 with pneumatic tires (1940)
Nebraska test number	333 and 334

Numbers produced (includes HV)
1939	na
1940	41,317
1941	40,927
1942	34,987

1943	21,375
1944	37,265
1945	28,268
1946	25,615
1947	28,382
1948	32,265
1949	27,483
1950	24,681
1951	24,232
1952	16,243
1953	21,916 (probably includes some Super Hs)

390,317 Farmall Hs produced

Serial numbers

1939	501–10652
1940	10653–52386
1941	52387–93236
1942	93237–122589
1943	122590–150250
1944	150251–186122
1945	186123–214819
1946	214820–241142
1947	241143–268990
1948	268991–300875
1949	300876–327974
1950	327975–351922
1951	351923–375860
1952	375861–390499
1953	390500–391730
Chassis prefixes	FBH
Engine prefixes	FBHM
Chassis serial number location	stamped on plate, left side of clutch housing
Engine serial number location	right side of engine crankcase above ignition unit

Regular Equipment

Distillate or high-compression gasoline engine optional, distillate-engine tractor included radiator shutter and heat indicator, IH magneto, variable-speed governor, oil-bath air cleaner, large upholstered seat, foot-operated differential brakes, and quick-attachable drawbar

Attachments and Special Features

Air pipe extension, belt pulley attachment, collector pre-cleaner, cultivator shifter lever, high-compression gasoline attachment, kerosene attachment, exhaust muffler, exhaust pipe extension, adjustable wide-tread front axle, single front wheel for 7.50x10 tire, single front wheel for

6.50x16 tire, wheel weights, special fuel tank with fuel trap, heat indicator for conventional radiator, heat indicator for pressurized radiator, reverse-flow radiator fan, hydraulic Lift-All attachment, low-boiling-point thermostat for conventional radiator, overtires for steel wheels, pintle-hook drawbar, 5,000- and 8,000-foot high-altitude pistons for both gasoline and kerosene engines, rear PTO, radiator shutter, 100-inch wide-tread rear axle, right rear axle extension, rear wheel fenders, channel rim (rear wheels), heavy steel (rear wheels), skid rings, spark arrester, low-low 1st gear (pneumatic tires only), 7-mph 4th gear (pneumatic tires only), swinging drawbar, tire pump, variable-tread front wheels, Bosch "No Battery" lighting attachment, Delco-Remy lighting attachment, Delco-Remy starting attachment, Delco-Remy starting and lighting attachment, lighting attachment for tractors with starting attachment, distillate engine, magneto ignition (later tractors, standard earlier), and hour meter

Major Changes/Dates

First tractor (FBH 501) built July 3, 1939
First high-compression gasoline tractor (FBH 20891 X1) built March 29, 1940
H discontinued January 26, 1953

Comments

None

Farmall HV

Engine	C-152
Cylinders	four
Bore and stroke	3 3/8x4 1/4 inches
Displacement	152.1 cubic inches
Rated rpm	1,000–1,650
Compression ratio	5.9:1
Ignition	IH H-4 magneto
Carburetor	1-inch IH D-10 updraft
Cooling capacity	4 1/8 gallons
Fuel tank capacity	17 1/2 gallons, 7/8 gallon starting (diesel and kerosene versions)

Horsepower ratings

Drawbar	25
PTO/belt	27.5
Length	146 inches
Wheelbase	91 inches
Height	87 1/4 inches
Width	85 7/8 inches at ends of rear axle
Available treads	69 inches rear; 60, 63, and 66 inches (front)
Weight	4,775 pounds

Speed, forward, 9.00x36 tires

Gear ....Speed
1 ....2 mph
2 ....3 3/8 mph
3 ....4 mph
4 ....5 mph
5 ....15 1/4 mph
Reverse ....2 7/8 mph
Price $2,740 (1951)
Nebraska test number....................................na
Numbers produced.......................................863
Serial numbers ....see Farmall H listing
Chassis prefixes ....FBHV
Engine prefixes...FBHVM
Chassis serial number location ....plate on left side of clutch housing
Engine serial number location.......................right side of crankcase above ignition unit

Regular Equipment

Choice of either distillate or high-compression gasoline engine, IH magneto, water pump, oil-type air cleaner, large upholstered seat, foot brakes, flat-bar-type drawbar, 6.00x20 front tires, and 9.00x36 cane-type rear tires

Attachments and Special Features

Air pipe extension, belt pulley attachment, collector pre-cleaner, cultivator shifter lever, high-compression gasoline attachment, kerosene attachment, exhaust muffler, exhaust pipe extension, wheel weights, special fuel tank with fuel trap, heat indicator for conventional radiator, heat indicator for pressurized radiator, hydraulic Lift-All attachment, low-boiling-point thermostat for conventional radiator, overtires for steel wheels, 5,000- and 8,000-foot high-altitude pistons for both gasoline and kerosene engines, rear PTO, radiator shutter, rear wheel fenders, spark arrester, tire pump, Bosch "No Battery" lighting attachment, Delco-Remy lighting attachment, Delco-Remy starting attachment, Delco-Remy starting and lighting attachment, and lighting attachment for tractors with starting attachments

Major Changes/Dates

Production authorized January 29, 1942
Discontinued February 3, 1953

Comments

None

Farmall Super H

Engine..C-164
Cylinders ....four
Bore and stroke...3 1/2x4 1/4 inches

FARMALL SUPER H
This is a later Super H with live hydraulics. There are two distinct types of Super Hs, distinguishable by whether the tractor has the old transmission-driven hydraulics or the newer engine-driven hydraulics. *State Historical Society of Wisconsin*

Displacement	164 cubic inches
Rated rpm	900–1,650
Compression ratio	6.1:1
Ignition	6-volt battery
Carburetor	1 1/4-inch IH updraft
Cooling capacity	4 1/8 gallons
Fuel tank capacity	17 gallons
Horsepower ratings	
Drawbar	31.04 (IH)
PTO/belt	34.61 (IH)
Length	133 inches
Wheelbase	89 1/4 inches
Height	85 inches (at top of muffler)
Width	75 inches
Available treads	48–88 inches (rear), 8 1/8 to 16 3/4 inches (front)
Weight	3,840 pounds without fluids
Speed, forward, 11.00x38 tires	
Gear	*Speed*
1	2 5/8 mph
2	3 3/4 mph
3	5 mph
4	6 5/8 mph
5	16 1/4 mph
Reverse	3 1/4 mph
Price	na
Nebraska test number	492

Numbers produced
    1953 21,916
    1954 10,052
    28,691 Farmall Super Hs produced
Serial numbers (includes Super HV)
    1953 ....501–22201 (some probably were
                          regular Hs)
    1954 22202–29285
Chassis prefixes ....SH
Engine prefixes...C-164
Chassis serial number location ....left side of clutch housing
Engine serial number location........................right side of engine above crankcase
                                       breather

Regular Equipment

Deluxe hydraulic seat, swinging drawbar, electric starter and lights, muffler, variable-tread front wheels, PTO, belt pulley, hydraulic Lift-All (later tractors), heat indicator, and 11.00x38 rear tires and 5.50x16 front tires (10.00x38 and 12.00x38 rears and 6.00x16 front tires optional)

Attachments and Special Features

Hydraulic remote control, single front wheel, adjustable wide-tread front axle, 100-inch-tread rear axle, wheel weights, spark arrester, collector pre-cleaner, intake pipe extension, exhaust pipe extension, hour meter, service meter, engine tire pump, fenders, radiator shutter, high-altitude pistons, pre-cleaner, combination rear lamp and taillamp, magneto ignition, tilt-back feature for hydraulic seat, low-low-speed attachment giving 1 3/4 mph in 1st and 2 1/8 mph in reverse, steel wheels, other wheel and tire equipment, cultivator stay rod anchor bracket, hydraulic Lift-All (early tractors), live hydraulics (later tractors), and right rear axle extension.

Major Changes/Dates

Discontinued October 22, 1954

Comments

None

Farmall Super HV

Engine..C-164
Cylinders ....four
Bore and stroke ....3x4 1/4 inches
Displacement ....164 cubic inches
Rated rpm 1,650
Compression ratio...6.1:1
Ignition..6-volt battery
Carburetor...1 1/4-inch IH updraft
Cooling capacity ....4 1/8 gallons

LARGE FARMALL SERIAL NUMBER LOCATION

The larger Farmalls, starting with the H and M, have the chassis serial number plates mounted on the left side of the clutch housing, as seen here. The serial number plate Super H and H, 300 and 400, and the 350 and 450 are all in the same place. This plate was steam cleaned along with the rest of the tractor, which faded the paint.

FARMALL SUPER HV

The Super HV is a very rare tractor today, generally found only in certain sections of the country. The unique high-arched front axles, stay rods, hitch, and decal can all be seen here. The goal was to add crop clearance. *State Historical Society of Wisconsin*

Fuel tank capacity	17 gallons, 7/8 gallon starting
Horsepower ratings	
Drawbar	29 (IH)
PTO/belt	33 (IH)
Length	146 inches
Wheelbase	93 3/4 inches
Height	87 inches (at steering wheel)

Width ....85 7/8 inches
Available treads ....60–90 inches (front), 69 inches
                                                                 (rear)
Weight ....5,075 pounds
Speed, forward, 12.00x36 tires
   Gear...*Speed*
   1 ....2 mph
   2 ....3 mph
   3 ....4 3/4 mph
   4 ....6 3/8 mph
   5 ....15 3/8 mph
   Reverse ....3 1/8 mph
Price ....na
Nebraska test number.....................na
Numbers produced.........................70
Serial numbers ....see Farmall Super H listing
Chassis prefixes ....SHV
Engine prefixes...............................C-164
Chassis serial number location ......left side of clutch housing
Engine serial number location.......right side of engine above crankcase
                                                                 breather

Regular Equipment

Deluxe hydraulic seat, swinging drawbar, electric starter and lights, muffler, variable-tread front wheels, PTO, belt pulley, hydraulic Lift-All, and heat indicator

Attachments and Special Features

Auxiliary stay rods, quick-attachable high-hitch heavy-duty drawbar, hydraulic remote control, wheel weights, spark arrester, collector pre-cleaner, intake pipe extension, exhaust pipe extension, hour meter, service meter, engine tire pump, fenders, radiator shutter, high-altitude pistons, pre-cleaner, combination rear lamp and taillamp, magneto ignition, and tilt-back feature for hydraulic seat

Major Changes/Dates

Discontinued October 22, 1954

Comments

Gives 30 1/4 inches crop clearance under front axles. No attempt made to match engine and chassis serial numbers.

Farmall M

Engine C-248
Cylinders ....four
Bore and stroke.............................3 7/8x5 1/4 inches
Displacement ....247.7 cubic inches

FARMALL M
The Farmall M is the largest member of the Farmall letter series and one of the most popular tractors for today's collector. This one has a wide front end instead of the more popular (in its time) narrow front. *State Historical Society of Wisconsin*

Rated rpm	950–1,450
Compression ratio	5.65:1
Ignition	IH H-4 magneto
Carburetor	1 1/4-inch IH E-12 updraft
Cooling capacity	6 gallons
Fuel tank capacity	21 gallons, 7/8 gallon starting
Horsepower ratings	
Drawbar	34.44 gasoline, 32.86 distillate (IH)
PTO/belt	39.23 gasoline, 36.70 distillate (IH)
Length	133 1/8 inches
Wheelbase	88 3/4 inches
Height	78 1/4 inches (at steering wheel)
Width	100 inches (rear tires), 84 inches (rear axles)
Available treads	52–88 inches (rear), 8 3/8 inches (front)
Weight	4,910 pounds with Lift-All and other equipment

Speed, forward, 11.00x38 tires

Gear	Speed
1	2 5/8 mph
2	3 mph
3	4 1/4 mph
4	5 1/8 mph

```
5 .......................................................16 3/8 mph
Reverse ...............................................3 1/8 mph
```

Price (1940) ....$895 steel, $1,070 pneumatic
Nebraska test number....................................327 and 328

Numbers produced (includes M, MV, and MDV)

```
1939 ......................................................na
1940 ......................................................19,190
1941 ......................................................23,387
1942 ......................................................12,921
1943 ......................................................4,789
1944 ......................................................20,338
1945 ......................................................7,606
1946 ......................................................15,763
1947 ......................................................26,321
1948 ......................................................28,641
1949 ......................................................33,166
1950 ......................................................35,373
1951 ......................................................41,381
1952 ......................................................30,056 (some Super Ms)
```

270,140 Farmall Ms produced

Serial numbers

```
1939 ......................................................501–7239
1940 ......................................................7240–25370
1941 ......................................................25371–50987
1942 ......................................................50988–60010
1943 ......................................................60011–67423
1944 ......................................................67424–88084
1945 ......................................................88085–105563 or 88085–104214
1946 ......................................................105564–122822 or 104215–114205
1947 ......................................................122823–151807 or 114206–149769
1948 ......................................................151708–180513 or 149700–177219
1949 ......................................................180514–213578 or 177220–212736
1950 ......................................................213579–247517 or 212737–247517
1951 ......................................................247518–290922 or 247518–285099
1952 ......................................................290923–298218 or 285100–298218
```

Chassis prefixes ....FBK
Engine prefixes...FBKM
Chassis serial number location ....left side of clutch housing
Engine serial number location......................pad on right side of crankcase

Regular Equipment

Choice of high-compression gasoline or distillate engine (distillate includes radiator shutter and heat indicator), IH magneto, large upholstered seat, quick-attachable drawbar, foot-operated brakes, and 51-inch rear steel wheels and 22-inch steel front wheels (1940)

Attachments and Special Features

Radiator shutter, heat indicator, 5,000- and 8,000-foot high-altitude pistons, exhaust muffler, exhaust pipe extension, spark arrester, air pipe extension, collector pre-cleaner, swinging drawbar, adjustable drawbar, PTO, belt pulley, tire pump, electric starting and lighting, wheel weights, adjustable-tread wide front axle with adjustable wheelbase, variable-tread pneumatic front wheels, 100-inch-tread rear axles, rear wheel fenders, overtires for steel wheels, rear wheel extension rims, spade lugs, single front wheel, reverse-flow fan, 7-mph 4th speed, low-low first speed (1 5/8 mph), and cultivator shifting lever

Major Changes/Dates

First production M (FBK 501) built July 3, 1939 (one source lists July 15, 1939)

First gasoline high-compression engine was FBK 18144

M discontinued March 27, 1952

Modified M discontinued April 7, 1952

M Cotton Picker discontinued April 8, 1952

Comments

None

Farmall MD

Engine	D-248
Cylinders	four
Bore and stroke	3 7/8x5 1/4 inches
Displacement	247.7 cubic inches
Rated rpm	800–1,450
Compression ratio	14.2:1
Ignition	IH H-4 magneto
Carburetor	IH F-8
Cooling capacity	7 gallons
Fuel tank capacity	21 gallons, 1 gallon starting
Horsepower ratings	
Drawbar	33
PTO/belt	36
Length	126 3/4 inches
Wheelbase	90 1/4 inches
Height	78 1/4 inches (at steering wheel)
Width	100 inches (wheels), 84 inches (rear axles)
Available treads	52–88 inches (rear), 8 3/8 inches (front)
Weight	5,285 pounds equipped with Lift-All, others

Speed, forward, 11.00x38 tires

Gear .... Speed
1 .... 2 5/8 mph
2 .... 3 mph
3 .... 4 1/4 mph
4 .... 5 1/8 mph
5 .... 16 3/8 mph
Reverse .... 3 1/8 mph
Price $3,145 (1951)
Nebraska test number .... 368 and 460
Numbers produced 18,253
Serial numbers .... see Farmall M listing
Chassis prefixes .... FDBK
Engine prefixes .... FDBKM
Chassis serial number location .... left side of clutch housing
Engine serial number location .... top milled section of left side of crankcase

Regular Equipment
Information not available

Attachments and Special Features
Radiator shutter, heat indicator, exhaust muffler, exhaust pipe extension, spark arrester, air pipe extension, collector pre-cleaner, swinging drawbar, adjustable drawbar, PTO, belt pulley, tire pump, electric starting and lighting, wheel weights, adjustable-tread wide front axle with adjustable wheelbase, variable-tread pneumatic front wheels, 100-inch-tread rear axles, rear wheel fenders, overtires for steel wheels, rear wheel extension rims, spade lugs, single front wheel, reverse-flow fan, 7-mph 4th speed, low-low first speed (1 5/8 mph), and cultivator shifting lever

Major Changes/Dates
First Model MD (FDBK 26145) built January 13, 1941
MD discontinued March 27, 1952
Modified MD discontinued April 7, 1952
MD Cotton Picker August 7, 1952

Comments
None

Farmall MV
Engine C-248
Cylinders .... four
Bore and stroke .... 3 7/8x5 1/4 inches
Displacement .... 247.7 cubic inches
Rated rpm 950–1,450

Compression ratio 5.65:1
Ignition...IH H-4
Carburetor..1 1/4-inch IH E-12 updraft
Cooling capacity ....6 gallons
Fuel tank capacity ....21 gallons, 7/8 gallon starting
Horsepower ratings
    Drawbar..33.5
    PTO/belt 38.5
Length..146 inches
Wheelbase..91 inches
Height ....90 1/4 inches
Width ....85 7/8 inches rear axles
Available treads ....69 inches rear; 60, 63, or 66
    inches (front)
Weight ....5,890 pounds, equipped
Speed, forward,10.00x36 tires
    Gear..*Speed*
    1 ....2 mph
    2 ....3 3/8 mph
    3 ....4 1/8 mph
    4 ....5 mph
    5 ....16 mph
    Reverse ....3 1/8 mph
Price $3,102 (1951)
Nebraska test number....................................na
Numbers produced...1,674
Serial numbers ....see Farmall M listing
Chassis prefixes ....MV-FBKV
Engine prefixes...FBKVM
Chassis serial number location ....left side of clutch housing
Engine serial number location.........................pad on right side of crankcase

Regular Equipment
    Choice of distillate (with radiator shutter and heat control) or high-compression gasoline engine, large upholstered seat, flat-bar-type draw-bar, 6.00x20 front tires, and 10.00x36 cane rear tires

Attachments and Special Features
    Air pipe extensions, belt pulley, cultivator shifter lever, electric starting and lighting, exhaust muffler, exhaust pipe extension, heat indicator, high-altitude pistons, PTO, collector-type pre-cleaner, radiator shutter, rear wheel fenders, wheel weights, spark arrester, tire pump, and hydraulic Lift-All

Major Changes/Dates
    Production authorized January 29, 1942
    Discontinued March 28, 1952

Comments
None

Farmall MDV

Engine D-248
Cylinders ....four
Bore and stroke ....3 7/8x5 1/4 inches
Displacement ....247.7 cubic inches
Rated rpm 1,450
Compression ratio 14.2:1
Ignition...IH H-4 magneto
Carburetor...IH F-8
Cooling capacity ....6 3/4 gallons
Fuel tank capacity ....21 gallons, 7/8 gallon starting
Horsepower ratings
    Drawbar.....................................31.5
    PTO/belt 36
Length..148 inches
Wheelbase..93 inches
Height ....90 1/4 inches
Width ....85 7/8 inches rear axles
Available treads ....69 inches rear; 60, 63, or 66 inches
    (front)
Weight ....6,265 pounds, equipped
Speed, forward, 10.00x36 tires
    Gear ....*Speed*
    1 ....2 mph
    2 ....3 3/8 mph
    3 ....4 1/8 mph
    4 ....5 mph
    5 ....16 mph
    Reverse ....3 1/8 mph
Price $3,901 (1951)
Nebraska test number..................... na
Numbers produced............................509
Serial numbers ....see Farmall M listing
Chassis prefixes ....FDBKV
Engine prefixes..................................FDBKVM
Chassis serial number location ....left side of clutch housing
Engine serial number location...........top milled section of left side of
    crankcase

Regular Equipment
Diesel engine, large upholstered seat, flat-bar-type drawbar, 6.00x20 front tires, and 10.00x36 cane rear tires

Attachments and Special Features

Air pipe extensions, belt pulley, cultivator shifter lever, electric starting and lighting, exhaust muffler, exhaust pipe extension, heat indicator, PTO, collector-type pre-cleaner, radiator shutter, rear wheel fenders, wheel weights, spark arrester, tire pump, and hydraulic Lift-All

Major Changes/Dates

Production authorized September 4, 1942
Discontinued April 21, 1952

Comments

None

Farmall Super M

Engine	C-264 vertical inline, removable sleeves, overhead valves
Cylinders	four
Bore and stroke	4x5 1/4 inches
Displacement	264 cubic inches
Rated rpm	1,450
Compression ratio	5.9:1 (aluminum pistons), 6.75:1 (LPG)
Ignition	6-volt battery
Carburetor	1 1/4-inch IH updraft (gasoline, kerosene, distillate) or 1 1/4-inch Ensign X-9 (LPG)
Cooling capacity	6 1/4 gallons
Fuel tank capacity	21 gallons, 7/8 gallon starting
Horsepower ratings	
Drawbar	42 gasoline, 36 distillate
PTO/belt	47.5 gasoline, 41 distillate
Length	134 5/8 inches
Wheelbase	89 1/4 inches
Height	79 inches
Width	101 1/4 inches (rear wheels), 84 inches (rear axles)
Available treads	52–88 inches (rear); 8 3/8, 12 1/4, 13 5/8, or 17 inches (front)
Weight	5,100 pounds
Speed	

Gear	Speed
1	2 5/8 mph
2	3 3/4 mph
3	5 mph
4	6 3/4 mph
5	16 3/4 mph
Reverse	3 5/8 mph

FARMALL SUPER M
The Super M, an extremely popular tractor in its day, was an improved power version of the M. *State Historical Society of Wisconsin*

Price ....na
Nebraska test number.....................................475
Numbers produced (includes Super MD, Super MDV, Super MV)
   1952...30,056 (includes some regular Ms)
   1953...45,543
   1954...26,924 (mostly Super MTA)
  44,551 Farmall Super Ms produced
Serial numbers
  Farmall
     1952...501–12515
     1953...12516–51976
     1954...51977–52627
  Louisville
     1952...500001–501905
     1953...501906–512541 or 512540
     1954...512541–up
Chassis prefixes ....SM ("L" added to end for Louisville production)
Engine prefixes...C-264
Chassis serial number location ....stamped on plate on left side of clutch housing
Engine serial number location........................right side of engine on pad located above battery ignition unit

Regular Equipment
    Gas engine with battery ignition and exhaust valve rotators, starter and lights, muffler, Lift-All, hydraulic deluxe foam rubber seat, variable-tread front wheels, swinging drawbar, belt pulleys, PTO, heat indicator, 6.00x16 front tires, and 12.00x38 rear tires (alternatives available)

Attachments and Special Features
    LPG and distillate engines, magneto ignition, fenders, adjustable-tread front axle, wide-tread rear axle, single front wheel, spring-mounted seat jute or foam rubber padded, hour meter, service meter, high-altitude pistons, radiator shutter, remote control, wheel weights, intake extension, exhaust extension, collector pre-cleaner, pre-screener, spark arrester, and dual rear lamp

Farmall Super MD
The Super MD had the familiar IH start-on-gas diesel engine, as did its predecessor, the MD. These tractors are rarer than the gas versions but are also more expensive and complicated to restore. *State Historical Society of Wisconsin*

Major Changes/Dates
Super M discontinued February 1, 1954
Modified Super M discontinued March 25, 1954

Comments
No attempt made at factory to match engine and chassis serial numbers

Farmall Super MD

Engine	D-264
Cylinders	four
Bore and stroke	4x5 1/4 inches
Displacement	264 cubic inches
Rated rpm	900–1,450
Compression ratio	16.5:1
Ignition	12-volt battery (gas start)
Carburetor	IH F-8 (gas start)
Cooling capacity	7 gallons
Fuel tank capacity	20 1/2 gallons, 7/8 gallon starting
Horsepower ratings	
Drawbar	42
PTO/belt	47.5
Length	136 1/8 inches
Wheelbase	90 3/4 inches
Height	79 inches
Width	101 1/4 inches (rear wheels), 84 inches (rear axles)
Available treads	52–88 inches (rear); 8 1/8, 12 1/4, 13 5/8, or 17 inches (front)
Weight	5,485 pounds

Speed

Gear	Speed
1	2 5/8 mph
2	3 3/4 mph
3	5 mph
4	6 3/4 mph
5	16 3/4 mph
Reverse	3 5/8 mph

Price ....na
Nebraska test number....................................477 and 484 (LPG)
Numbers produced..5,199
Serial numbers ....see Farmall Super M listing
Chassis prefixes ....SMD ("L" added for Louisville production)
Engine prefixes...D-264
Chassis serial number location ....stamped on nameplate on left side of clutch housing
Engine serial number location.......................stamped on left side of engine crankcase above injection pump

Regular Equipment
Diesel engine with battery ignition for starting, starter and lights, muffler, Lift-All, hydraulic deluxe foam rubber seat, variable-tread front wheels, swinging drawbar, belt pulleys, PTO, heat indicator, 6.00x16 front tires, and 12.00x38 rear tires

Attachments and Special Features
Magneto ignition, fenders, adjustable wide-tread front axle, wide-tread rear axle, single front wheel, spring-mounted seat jute or foam rubber padded, hour meter, service meter, radiator shutter, remote control, wheel weights, intake extension, exhaust extension, collector pre-cleaner, pre-screener, spark arrester, and dual rear lamp

Major Changes/Dates
Super MD discontinued February 1, 1954
Super MDCH discontinued June 8, 1954

Comments
No attempt was made by the factory to match engine and tractor serial numbers

Farmall Super MV
Engine C-264
Cylinders ....four
Bore and stroke..4x5 1/4 inches
Displacement ....264 cubic inches
Rated rpm 1,450

Compression ratio..5.9:1 (aluminum pistons), 6.75:1 (LPG)
Ignition...6-volt battery
Carburetor..1 1/4-inch IH updraft (gasoline, kerosene, and distillate) or 1 1/4-inch Ensign X-9 (LPG)
Cooling capacity ....6 1/4 gallons
Fuel tank capacity ....21 gallons, 7/8 gallon
Horsepower ratings
   Drawbar..41 gasoline, 35.5 distillate
   PTO/belt...47.5 gasoline, 41 distillate
Length...146 inches
Wheelbase..91 inches
Height ....90 inches
Width ....85 7/8 inches ends of rear axles
Available treads ....69 inches (rear); 60, 63, or 66 inches (front)
Weight ....6,075 pounds
Speed

Gear	Speed
1	2 3/4 mph
2	3 7/8 mph
3	5 mph
4	6 7/8 mph
5	16 7/8 mph
Reverse	3 5/8 mph

Price ....na
Nebraska test number.....................................na
Numbers produced...245
Serial numbers ....see Farmall Super M listing
Chassis prefixes ....SMV ("L" added for Louisville production)
Engine prefixes..C-264
Chassis serial number location ....left side of clutch housing
Engine serial number location............................right side of engine above ignition unit

Regular Equipment

Gasoline engine with battery ignition and valve rotators, starter and lights, muffler, Lift-All, hydraulic deluxe foam rubber seat, variable-tread front wheels, PTO, heat indicator, 6.00x20 front wheels, and 13.00x36 cane-field-type rear wheels

Attachments and Special Features

Distillate engine, LPG engine, magneto ignition, fenders, variable-tread rear rims, belt pulley, high-hitch drawbar, spring-mounted seat foam rubber or jute padded, hour meter, radiator shutter, high-altitude pistons, remote control, wheel weights, intake extension, exhaust extension, collector pre-cleaner, pre-screener, spark arrester, and dual rear lamps

Major Changes/Dates
Discontinued March 1, 1954

Comments
None

Farmall Super MDV

Engine	D-264
Cylinders	four
Bore and stroke	4x5 1/4 inches
Displacement	264 cubic inches
Rated rpm	1,450
Compression ratio	16.5:1
Ignition	12-volt battery (gas start)
Carburetor	IH F-8 (gas start)
Cooling capacity	7 gallons
Fuel tank capacity	20 1/2 gallons, 7/8 gallon starting
Horsepower ratings	
Drawbar	41 (IH)
PTO/belt	47.5 (IH)
Length	148 inches
Wheelbase	93 1/8 inches
Height	90 inches (top of steering wheel)
Width	85 7/8 inches (ends of rear axles)
Available treads	69 inches (rear); 60, 63, or 66 inches (front)
Weight	6,450 pounds
Speed	

Gear	Speed
1	2 3/4 mph
2	3 7/8 mph
3	5 mph
4	6 7/8 mph
5	16 7/8 mph
Reverse	3 5/8 mph

Price	na
Nebraska test number	na
Numbers produced	89
Serial numbers	see Farmall Super M listing
Chassis prefixes	SMDV ("L" added for Louisville production)
Engine prefixes	D-264
Chassis serial number location	stamped on name tag, left side of clutch housing

Engine serial number location.......................left side of engine above injection pump

Regular Equipment

Diesel engine with battery ignition for starting, starter and lights, muffler, Lift-All, hydraulic deluxe foam rubber seat, variable-tread front wheels, PTO, heat indicator, 6.00x20 front wheels, and 13.00x36 cane-field-type rear wheels

Attachments and Special Features

Magneto ignition, fenders, variable-tread rear rims, belt pulley, high-hitch drawbar, spring-mounted seat foam rubber or jute padded, hour meter, radiator shutter, remote control, wheel weights, intake extension, exhaust extension, collector pre-cleaner, pre-screener, spark arrester, dual rear lamp, belt pulley, and PTO

Major Changes/Dates

Discontinued March 24, 1954

Comments

No attempt was made by the factory to match engine and chassis serial numbers

Farmall Super M-TA

Engine..C-264
Cylinders ....four
Bore and stroke...............................4x5 1/4 inches
Displacement ....264 cubic inches
Rated rpm 1,600
Compression ratio...........................5.9:1
Ignition...6-volt battery
Carburetor ....1 1/4-inch IH updraft or Ensign X-9 (LPG)
Cooling capacity ....6 1/4 gallons
Fuel tank capacity ....21 gallons, 7/8 gallon starting
Horsepower ratings.........................na
Length..145 inches
Wheelbase......................................99 3/4 inches
Height ....79 inches (at steering wheel)
Width ....84 inches (rear axles), 101 1/4 inches (rear wheels)
Available treads ....8 3/8, 12 1/4, 13 5/8, or 17 inches (front); 57–89 inches (rear)
Weight ....na
Speed, forward, 12.00x38 tires
    Gear.........................Speed
    ....<u>Regular</u>...................... <u>Torque Amplifier</u>

Farmall Super M-TA
The Super M-TA is distinguishable by its more complicated clutch linkages, located on the left side of the clutch housing (except for those rare versions built without the Torque Amplifier). The Torque Amplifier version featured an auxiliary planetary gearset that doubled the number of gears and allowed downshifting to a lower gear without stopping the tractor. *State Historical Society of Wisconsin*

1	2 mph	1 5/8 mph
2	3 7/8 mph	2 5/8 mph
3	4 7/8 mph	3 1/4 mph
4	6 3/4 mph	4 mph
5	16 3/4 mph	11 1/4 mph
Reverse	3 3/8 mph	2 1/4 mph

Price ....na
Nebraska test number....................................na
Numbers produced..26,924 (1954)
Serial numbers 60001–83523 (1954)
Chassis prefixes ....SM-TA
Engine prefixes..C-264
Chassis serial number location ....left side of clutch housing
Engine serial number location.......................right side of engine above ignition

Regular Equipment
Information not available

Attachments and Special Features
Kerosene, distillate, and LPG engines; TA; independent PTO; air pipe extension; belt pulley; combination rear light and taillight; cultivator stay rod anchor bracket; swinging drawbar; engine hour meter; exhaust muffler; exhaust pipe extension; Farmall Lift-All; fenders; adjustable wide-

tread front axle; 5- and 8-foot hydraulic hose extensions; 5,000-foot high-altitude pistons for kerosene and distillate; 5,000-foot pistons for gasoline; 8,000-foot high-altitude pistons for kerosene and distillate; 8,000-foot pistons for gasoline; transmission-driven PTO; pre-cleaner (collector or detachable sleeve types); pre-screener; radiator shutter; 100-inch-tread rear axle; rear axle extension for sugar beet harvester; remote-control cylinder package; remote-control tractor attachment; deluxe upholstered seat; detachable seat pad; deluxe detachable seat pad; heavy operator seat spring; medium operator seat spring; service meter; spark arrester; tilt-back seat bracket; Engineair tire pump; Schrader tire pump; Schrader tire pump kit; and a variety of wheels and tires, steel wheels, and wheel weights

Major Changes/Dates
Discontinued October 15, 1954

Comments
No attempt was made by the factory to match engine and chassis serial numbers

Farmall Super MD-TA

Engine	D-264
Cylinders	four
Bore and stroke	4x5 1/4 inches
Displacement	264 cubic inches
Rated rpm	na
Compression ratio	16.5:1
Ignition	12-volt battery (gas start)
Carburetor	IH F-8 (gas start)
Cooling capacity	7 gallons
Fuel tank capacity	20 1/2 gallons, 7/8 gallon starting
Horsepower ratings	na
Length	145 inches
Wheelbase	99 3/4 inches
Height	79 inches (at steering wheel)
Width	84 inches (over rear axles), 101 1/4 inches (with rear wheels out)
Available treads	8 3/8, 12 1/4, 13 5/8, or 17 inches (front); 57–89 inches (rear)
Weight	na

Speed

Gear	Speed Regular	Torque Amplifier
1	2 mph	1 5/8 mph
2	3 7/8 mph	2 5/8 mph
3	4 7/8 mph	3 1/4 mph
4	6 3/4 mph	4 mph

| 5 | 16 3/4 mph | 11 1/4 mph |
| Reverse | 3 3/8 mph | 2 1/4 mph |

Price ....na
Nebraska test number....................................na
Numbers produced...2,705
Serial numbers ....see Farmall Super M-TA listing
Chassis prefixes ....SM-TA
Engine prefixes...D-264
Chassis serial number location ....left side of clutch housing
Engine serial number location........................left side of engine above injection pump

Regular Equipment
Information not available

Attachments and Special Features
Independent PTO, TA, air pipe extension, belt pulley, combination rear light and taillight, cultivator stay rod anchor bracket, swinging drawbar, engine hour meter, exhaust muffler, exhaust pipe extension, Farmall Lift-All, fenders, adjustable wide front axle, 5- and 8-foot hydraulic extensions, transmission-driven PTO, pre-cleaner (collector or detachable sleeve types), pre-screener, radiator shutter, 100-inch-tread rear axle, rear axle extension, deluxe upholstered seat, detachable seat pad, deluxe detachable seat pad, heavy operator seat spring, medium operator seat spring, service meter, spark arrester, tilt-back seat bracket, Engineair tire pump, Schrader tire pump, Schrader tire pump kit, and a variety of wheel and tire equipment, steel wheels, and wheel weights

Major Changes/Dates
Discontinued November 1, 1954

Comments
No attempt was made by the factory to match engine and chassis serial numbers

Farmall Super MV-TA

Engine C-264
Cylinders ....four
Bore and stroke..4x5 1/4 inches
Displacement ....264 cubic inches
Rated rpm 1,600
Compression ratio 5.9:1
Ignition...6-volt battery
Carburetor..1 1/4-inch IH updraft or Ensign X-9 (LPG)
Cooling capacity ....6 1/4 gallons
Fuel tank capacity ....21 gallons

FARMALL SUPER MV-TA

Horsepower ratings...na
Length...155 inches
Wheelbase...100 1/4 inches
Height ....90 inches (at steering wheel)
Width ....85 7/8 inches
Available treads ....60–84 inches (front), 69 inches
(rear)
Weight ....na
Speed

Gear	Speed Regular	Torque Amplifier
1	2 mph	1 3/4 mph
2	3 7/8 mph	2 5/8 mph
3	4 7/8 mph	3 1/4 mph
4	6 3/4 mph	4 5/8 mph
5	16 7/8 mph	11 3/8 mph
Reverse	3 3/8 mph	2 1/4 mph

Price ....na
Nebraska test number....................................na
Numbers produced...64
Serial numbers ....see Farmall Super M-TA listing
Chassis prefixes ....SM-TAV
Engine prefixes...C-264
Chassis serial number location ....left side of clutch housing
Engine serial number location.......................right side of engine above ignition
unit

Regular Equipment
Information not available

Attachments and Special Features
Kerosene, distillate, and LPG engines; TA; independent PTO; air pipe extension; auxiliary stay rods; belt pulley; combination rear light and taillight; quick-attachable high-hitch heavy-duty drawbar; engine hour meter; exhaust muffler; exhaust pipe extension; Farmall Lift-All extension; fenders; 5- and 8-foot hydraulic hose extensions; 5,000-foot altitude pistons for kerosene and distillate; 5,000-foot pistons for gasoline; 8,000-foot high-altitude pistons for kerosene and distillate; 8,000-foot pistons for gasoline; transmission-driven PTO; pre-cleaner (collector or detachable sleeve types); pre-screener; radiator shutter; remote-control cylinder package; remote-control tractor attachment; deluxe upholstered seat; detachable seat pad; deluxe detachable seat pad; heavy operator seat spring; medium operator seat spring; service meter; spark arrester; tilt-back seat bracket; Engineair tire pump; Schrader tire pump; Schrader tire pump kit; and wheel weights

Major Changes/Dates
Discontinued December 2, 1954

Comments
Speeds may be inaccurate; no attempt was made by the factory to match engine and chassis serial numbers

Farmall Super MDV-TA

Engine D-264
Cylinders ....four
Bore and stroke ....4x5 1/4 inches
Displacement ....264 cubic inches
Rated rpm ....na
Compression ratio...16.5:1
Ignition...12-volt battery (gas start)
Carburetor..IH F-8 (gas start)
Cooling capacity ....7 gallons
Fuel tank capacity ....20 gallons, 7/8 gallon starting
Horsepower ratings.......................................na
Length..155 inches
Wheelbase..100 1/4 inches
Height ....90 inches (at steering wheel)
Width ....85 7/8 inches rear axle
Available treads ....60–84 inches (front), 69 inches (rear)
Weight ....na
Speed

Gear	Speed
1	2 3/8 mph
2	3 5/8 mph
3	4 5/8 mph
4	6 3/8 mph
5	15 7/8 mph
Reverse	3 1/8 mph

Price ....na
Nebraska test number...................................na
Numbers produced..na
Serial numbers ....see Farmall Super M-TA listing
Chassis prefixes ....SM-TADV
Engine prefixes...D-264
Chassis serial number location ....left side of clutch housing
Engine serial number location..................left side of engine above injection pump

Regular Equipment
Information not available

Attachments and Special Features

Independent PTO; TA; air pipe extension; auxiliary stay rods; belt pulley; combination rear light and taillight; quick-attachable, high-hitch; heavy-duty drawbar; engine hour meter; exhaust muffler; exhaust pipe extension; Farmall Lift-All; fenders; 5- and 8-foot hydraulic extensions; transmission-driven PTO; pre-cleaner (collector or detachable sleeve types); pre-screener; radiator shutter; deluxe upholstered seat; detachable seat pad; deluxe detachable seat pad; heavy operator seat spring; medium operator seat spring; service meter; spark arrester; tilt-back seat bracket; Engineair tire pump; Schrader tire pump; Schrader tire pump kit; variety of wheel and tire equipment, steel wheels, and wheel weights

Major Changes/Dates

Discontinued January 25, 1955

Comments

No attempt was made by the factory to match engine and chassis serial numbers

Farmall Cub

Engine	C-60 vertical inline, L-head, sleeveless
Cylinders	four
Bore and stroke	2 5/8x2 3/4 inches
Displacement	59.5 cubic inches
Rated rpm	1,600
Compression ratio	6.5:1
Ignition	IH J-4 magneto
Carburetor	3/4-inch IH updraft
Cooling capacity	9 3/4 quarts
Fuel tank capacity	7 gallons
Horsepower ratings	

FARMALL CUB
The Farmall Cub was introduced in 1947 as a tractor to replace the horse on the very smallest of farms. These tractors were built in one form or another until 1979 and are extremely popular today. *State Historical Society of Wisconsin*

Drawbar...8.89 (IH)
PTO/belt ....9.76 (IH)
Length..99 3/8 inches
Wheelbase..69 1/4 inches
Height ....62 3/4 inches (top of steering
                                                                      wheel)
Width ....64 1/4 inches (max, wheels set
                                                                      out), 48 inches (ends of rear axle)
Available treads ....40–56 inches (rear), 40 5/8 inches
                                                                      and 46 3/8 inches (front)
Weight ....1,430 pounds (common field
                                                                      weight)

Speed

Gear	Speed
1	2 1/8 mph
2	3 1/8 mph
3	6 mph
Reverse	2 3/8 mph

Price $905 (1954)
Nebraska test number...................................386 and 575
Numbers produced

Year	Produced
1947	5,564
1948	43,040
1949	44,544
1950	23,421
1951	24,298
1952	17,691
1953	18,827
1954	4,242
1955	7,776
1956	5,023
1957	5,594

CUB SERIAL NUMBER LOCATION
The Cub serial number plates are among the easiest to find (and photograph), being located on the right side of the tractor next to the steering gear.

1958 3,794
Serial numbers
1947 501–11347
1948 11348–57830
1949 57831–99535
1950 99536–121453
1951 121454–144454
1952 144455–162283
1953 162284–179411
1954 179412–186440
1955 186441–193657
1956 ....193658–198230 or 198231
1957 198231–204388
1958 ....204389–211440 (Cub production
                                                                   continued in some form until 1979)
Chassis prefixes ....FCUB
Engine prefixes...FCUBM
Chassis serial number location ....plate on right side of steering gear
                                                                   housing
Engine serial number location......................left side of crankcase, right of carbu-
                                                                   retor

Regular Equipment
Magneto ignition, reversible drawbar, nonadjustable front axle, fenders, 3.00x12 front tires, and 6.00x24 rear tires

Attachments and Special Features
Battery ignition and electric starting and lighting, electric starting and lighting for magneto-equipped tractors, foam rubber upholstered seat, adjustable front axle, wide-tread increased-clearance attachment, swinging drawbar, PTO, PTO and belt pulley, hydraulic Touch Control, dual rear lamp, spark arrester, wheel weights, muffler, high-altitude cylinder head, exhaust and intake valve rotators, pneumatic tire pump, detachable seat pad, a variety of wheel and tire equipment, one-point Fast Hitch, and many additional features in later years

Major Changes/Dates
Information not available

Comments
Early 1950s models painted white

International Cub Low-Boy
Engine C-60
Cylinders ....four
Bore and stroke...2 5/8x2 3/4 inches
Displacement 59.5

Rated rpm 1,800
Compression ratio..6.5:1
Ignition..6-volt battery
Carburetor..3/4-inch IH updraft
Cooling capacity ....9 3/4 quarts
Fuel tank capacity ....7 gallons
Horsepower ratings
    Drawbar...9.4 (IH)
    PTO/belt...10.5 (IH)
Length...97 inches
Wheelbase..62 inches
Height ....55 1/4 inches (at steering wheel)
Width ....64 1/4 inches maximum, 48 1/4 inches minimum
Available treads ....front—nonadjustable axle 43 or 49 inches, adjustable axle 43–55 inches (4-inch intervals); rear—40–56 inches
Weight ....1,580 pounds
Speed

Gear	Speed
1	2.3 mph
2	3.1 mph
3	6.9 mph
Reverse	2.6 mph

Price ....na
Nebraska test number..................................na
Numbers produced
    1955 1,153
    1956 2,118
    1957 2,407
    1958 1,494
Serial numbers
    1955 501–2554
    1956 2555–3928
    1957 3929–6581
    1958 ....6582–10566 (Cub Lo-Boy produced until 1968)
Chassis prefixes ....IH Cub Lo-Boy
Engine prefixes...FCUBM
Chassis serial number location ....plate on right side of steering gear housing
Engine serial number location......................left hand of crankcase, right of carburetor

Regular Equipment
    Under-axle muffler, standard drawbar, nonadjustable front axle, magneto, non-upholstered pan seat, and 7.00x24 rear and 4.00x12 front tires

FARMALL C

The Farmall C was conceived as a replacement for the B, with adjustable rear axles. The result was a tractor that is remarkably pleasant to operate and very versatile. It does not have the dropped rear axle or the offset feature of the A or B. *State Historical Society of Wisconsin*

Attachments and Special Features

Fast Hitch, Touch Control, adjustable front axle, battery ignition, starter, lights, foam-rubber-padded pan seat, deluxe cushioned seat with padded back rest, arm rest pads for deluxe seat, vertically mounted exhaust muffler, PTO, belt pulley, combination rear lamp and taillight, swinging drawbar, exhaust valve rotators, spark arrester for vertical exhaust, wheel weights, fast-hitch cushion spring, horn, and safety lamp package

Major Changes/Dates

Information not available

Comments

None

Farmall C

Engine	C-113 or C-123 (late)
Cylinders	four
Bore and stroke	3x4 inches
Displacement	113 cubic inches, later 123 cubic inches
Rated rpm	1,650
Compression ratio	6.1:1
Ignition	IH H-4
Carburetor	Zenith 161x7, Marvel Schebler TSX-319 (gasoline), or Marvel Schebler TSX-333 (kerosene or distillate)
Cooling capacity	3 1/4 gallons
Fuel tank capacity	11 gallons
Horsepower ratings	
Drawbar	18.5 (IH)
PTO/belt	20.5 (IH)
Length	120 3/8 inches
Wheelbase	81 5/8 inches
Height	70 3/8 inches (at steering wheel)
Width	80 inches (rear axles)
Available treads	6 3/4 inches (front), 47–80 inches (rear)

Weight ....2,780 pounds without fuel or water
Speed
  Gear...*Speed*
  1 ....2 3/8 mph
  2 ....3 3/4 mph
  3 ....5 mph
  4 ....10 1/4 mph
  Reverse ....3 mph
Price ....na
Nebraska test number....................................395
Numbers produced
  1948 15,547
  1949 26,338
  1950 24,280
  1951 ....37,651 (includes some Super Cs)
Serial numbers
  1948 501–22623
  1949 22624–47009
  1950 47010–71879
  1951 71880–80432
Chassis prefixes ....FC
Engine prefixes...FCM
Chassis serial number location ....plate on tool box and seat support
Engine serial number location.......................right side of crankcase above ignition unit

Regular Equipment
  Gasoline or distillate engine, IH magneto, hydraulic seat, and adjustable swinging drawbar

Attachments and Special Features
  Touch Control, adjustable-tread double front wheels, adjustable wide-tread front axle, electric starter and lights, belt pulley, PTO, exhaust muffler, wheel weights, rear wheel fenders, pre-cleaner, air pipe extension, 88- and 100-inch-tread rear axles, single front wheel, radiator shutter, 5,000- and 8,000-foot pistons, tire pump, spark arrester, seed-plate, and fertilizer drive shafts

Major Changes/Dates
  Information not available

Comments
  Early 1950 models painted white

Farmall Super C
Engine..C-123, vertical inline
Cylinders ....four

FARMALL SUPER C
The Super C had a 123-cubic inch engine, as opposed to the C's 113-cubic inch engine. While it has more power, the Super C still retains the C's great mix of power, size, and utility. *State Historical Society of Wisconsin*

Bore and stroke	3x4 inches (kerosene), 3 1/8x4 inches (gasoline)
Displacement	123 cubic inches
Rated rpm	1,650
Compression ratio	6:1
Ignition	6-volt battery
Carburetor	Carter or Zenith 67x7
Cooling capacity	3 3/4 gallons
Fuel tank capacity	11 gallons
Horsepower ratings	
Drawbar	21.67 (IH)
PTO/belt	24.45
Length	123 inches
Wheelbase	82 1/4 inches
Height	74 3/4 inches
Width	90 3/4 inches (wheels), 80 inches (axles)
Available treads	48–71 inches or 57–80 inches (rear); 6 5/8, 9 3/8, 12 5/8 inches (front)
Weight	2,900 pounds (shipping weight)

Speed, forward, 10-36 tires

Gear	Speed
1	2 mph
2	3 7/8 mph
3	5 1/8 mph
4	10 5/8 mph
Reverse	3 1/8 mph

Price	$1,475 (1954)
Nebraska test number	458
Numbers produced	
1951	37,651
1952	31,130
1953	29,472

```
1954.................................................13,753
```
Serial numbers
```
1951 .........................................100001–131156
1952 .........................................131157–159129
1953 .........................................159130–187787
1954 .........................................187788–198310
```
Chassis prefixes ....FC
Engine prefixes..FCM
Chassis serial number location ....plate on tool box and seat support
Engine serial number location................................right side on engine above ignition unit

Regular Equipment

Gasoline engine, adjustable-tread double front wheels, swinging drawbar, hydraulic deluxe foam rubber seat, disc brakes, hydraulic Touch Control, belt pulley and PTO, muffler, heat indicator, exhaust valve rotators, starter and lights, battery ignition, and tire size as ordered

Attachments and Special Features

Distillate engine, magneto ignition, high-altitude pistons, fenders, nonadjustable front wheels, adjustable wide-tread front axle, single front wheel, wide-tread rear axles, air pipe extension, pre-screener, collector pre-cleaner, spark arrester, dual rear lamp, radiator shutter, remote control, exhaust valve rotators, Hydra-Creeper, Fast Hitch

Major Changes/Dates

Information not available

Comments

None

McCormick-Deering W-4

```
Engine..........................................C-152
Cylinders .....................................four
Bore and stroke............................3 3/8x4 1/4 inches
Displacement ...............................152 cubic inches
Maximum Rated rpm....................1,650
Compression ratio........................5.9:1
Ignition.........................................IH H-4 magneto
Carburetor....................................1-inch IH D-10 updraft
Cooling capacity ..........................4 1/4 gallons
Fuel tank capacity ........................17 gallons, 1 gallon starting
                                             (kerosene and distillate versions)
```
Horsepower ratings
```
    Drawbar..................................22.49 (IH)
    PTO/belt .................................24.87 (IH)
Length...........................................114 inches
Wheelbase.....................................66 5/8 inches
Height ...........................................80 inches
```

Width ....66 5/8 inches
Available Tread ....45 7/8 front, 52 rear
Weight ....3,890 pounds (regular equipment)
Speed, forward (W-4, 40-inch steel wheels)

Gear	Speed
1	2 3/8 mph
2	3 1/8 mph
3	4 mph
4	5 mph
5	14 mph (11-26 rubber)
Reverse	2 3/4 mph

Price ....na
Nebraska test number..................342 and 353
Numbers produced (all -4 series tractors)

Year	Number
1940	213
1941	2,741
1942	1,888
1943	1,759
1944	3,705
1945	2,799
1946	1,893
1947	2,822
1948	2,975
1949	2,973
1950	3,186
1951	3,519
1952	2,385
1953	2,566 (includes some Super-4 series)
1954	444

24,377 W-4s produced
Serial numbers

Year	Serial numbers
1940	501–942
1941	943–4055
1942	4056–5692
1943	5693–7592
1944	7593–11170
1945	11171–13933
1946	13934–16021
1947	16022–18879
1948	18880–21911
1949	21912–24469
1950	24470–28166
1951	28167–31213
1952	31214–33066
1953	33067–34176
1954	na

Chassis prefixes ....WBH
Engine prefixes.................................WBHM
Chassis serial number location ....nameplate on left side of clutch housing
Engine serial number location......................pad on right side of crankcase

Regular Equipment

Gasoline engine, pneumatic tires, magneto, heat indicator, front drawbar, adjustable flat-bar-type rear drawbar, and tilt-back waterproof upholstered seat (adjustable forward and back)

Attachments and Special Features

Air pipe extension, belt pulley attachment, collector pre-cleaner, high-compression gasoline attachment, kerosene attachment, exhaust muffler, exhaust pipe extension, front wheel weights (first and second sets), heat indicator for non-pressurized radiator, heat indicator for pressurized radiator, low-boiling-point thermostat and heat indicator for conventional radiator, overtires for steel wheels, pintle-hook drawbar, 5,000- and 8,000-foot high-altitude pistons for gasoline and kerosene engines, rear PTO, radiator shutter, skid rings, spark arrester, low-low first-speed attachment (pneumatic only), swinging drawbar, tire pump, Bosch "No Battery" lighting attachment, Delco-Remy starting attachment, Delco-Remy starting and lighting attachment, and lighting attachment (for tractors equipped with starting attachment

Major Changes/Dates

First W-4 (WBH 501) built February 12, 1940
Discontinued January 26, 1953

Comments

One IH serial list has production ending at 7586 in 1943 and 11165 in 1944

No attempt was made to match engine and chassis serial numbers

McCormick-Deering O-4

Engine C-152
Cylinders ....four
Bore and stroke ....3 3/8x4 1/4 inches
Displacement ....152.1 cubic inches
Rated rpm 1,000–1,650
Compression ratio...........................5.9:1
Ignition...IH H-4 magneto
Carburetor.....................................1-inch IH D-10 downdraft
Cooling capacity ....4 gallons
Fuel tank capacity ....17 gallons, 1 gallon starting
Horsepower ratings
    Drawbar...................................22 distillate (IH), 25 gasoline

PTO/belt	24 distillate (IH), 27.5 gasoline
Length	120 7/8 inches
Wheelbase	66 3/4 inches
Height	57 1/8 inches, 60 1/4 inches with steering wheel cowl
Width	60 1/4 inches
Available treads	45 7/8 inches (front), 41 3/4 inches (rear)
Weight	4,320 pounds

Speed, forward, 12.00x26 pneumatic tires

Gear	Speed
1	1 mph
2	3 1/8 mph
3	4 mph
4	5 mph
5	14 5/8 mph
Reverse	1 3/4 mph

Price	na
Nebraska test number	na
Numbers produced	2,721
Serial numbers	see W-4 listing
Chassis prefixes	OBH
Engine prefixes	OBHM
Chassis serial number location	plate on left side of clutch housing
Engine serial number location	pad on right side of crankcase

Regular Equipment

Gasoline engine, heat indicator, magneto, hand-operated single-plate over-center clutch, front drawbar, low-swinging adjustable drawbar, tilt-back waterproof upholstered seat, pneumatic tires, and Orchard fenders

Attachments and Special Features

Belt pulley attachment, high-compression gasoline attachment, kerosene attachment, distillate engine, first and second sets of front wheel weights, heat indicator for conventional radiator, heat indicator for pressurized radiator, low-boiling-point thermostat for conventional radiator, pintle-hook drawbar, 5,000- and 8,000-foot high-altitude pistons for both gasoline and kerosene engines, rear PTO, radiator shutter, first and second rear wheel weight sets, steering wheel cowl sheet, 7-mph 4th gear (pneumatic tires only), tire pump, Bosch "No Battery" lighting attachment, Delco-Remy lighting attachment, Delco-Remy starting attachment, Delco-Remy starting and lighting attachment, and steering wheel cowl

Major Changes/Dates

First kerosene-distillate O-4 (OBH 696 W3 [engine OBHM-501]) built October 1940

Comments

No attempt was made to match engine and chassis serial numbers

McCormick-Deering OS-4

Engine C-152
Cylinders ....four
Bore and stroke ....3 3/8x4 1/4 inches
Displacement ....152.1 cubic inches
Rated rpm 1,000–1,650
Compression ratio 5.9:1
Ignition..IH H-4 magneto
Carburetor..1-inch IH D-10 downdraft
Cooling capacity ....4 1/4 gallons
Fuel tank capacity ....17 1/2 gallons, 7/8 gallon starting
Horsepower ratings
    Drawbar..22 distillate, 25 starting
    PTO/belt ....24 distillate, 27.5 starting
Length...120 7/8 inches
Wheelbase...66 3/4 inches
Height ....57 1/8 inches (overall)
Width ....55 inches
Available treads ....45 7/8 inches (front), 41 3/4 inches (rear)
Weight ....4,120 pounds, equipped
Speed, forward, 12.00x26 tires

Gear	Speed
1	1 mph
2	3 1/8 mph
3	4 mph
4	5 mph
5	14 5/8 mph
Reverse	1 3/4 mph

Price $1,923 (1951)
Nebraska test number....................................na
Numbers produced...1,267
Serial numbers ....see W-4 listing
Chassis prefixes ....OBHS
Engine prefixes..OBHSM
Chassis serial number location ....plate on left side of clutch housing
Engine serial number location.......................pad on right side of crankcase

Regular Equipment

Gasoline engine, heat indicator, magneto, hand-operated single-plate over-center clutch, front drawbar, low-swinging adjustable drawbar, tilt-back waterproof upholstered seat, and pneumatic tires

Attachments and Special Features

Distillate engine, radiator shutter, belt pulleys, PTO, electric starting and lighting, wheel weights, 7-mph 4th gear, engine-operated tire pump, and 5,000- and 8,000-foot high-altitude pistons

Major Changes/Dates

Model OS-4 production authorized October 19, 1944, but the model was probably not produced until November 30, 1944

Discontinued January 13, 1954

Comments

None

International I-4

Engine	C-152
Cylinders	four
Bore and stroke	3 3/8x4 1/4 inches
Displacement	152.1 cubic inches
Rated rpm	1,650
Compression ratio	na
Ignition	IH H-4 magneto
Carburetor	1-inch IH D-10 updraft
Cooling capacity	4 1/4 gallons
Fuel tank capacity	17 gallons
Horsepower ratings	
Drawbar	25
PTO/belt	27.5
Length	113 3/4 inches
Wheelbase	66 3/4 inches
Height	62 3/4 inches
Width	58 7/8 inches
Available treads	45 7/8 inches (front), 46 1/8 inches (rear)
Weight	3,795 pounds

I-4

This I-4 is fitted with a grille guard and a Hough hydraulic end-loader. Hough was later purchased by IH. *State Historical Society of Wisconsin*

Speed, forward, 11.25x24 pneumatic tires

Gear	Speed
1	2 1/8 mph
2	3 mph
3	5 mph
4	7 mph
5	14 7/8 mph
Reverse	2 7/8 mph

Price	na
Nebraska test number	industrial tractors not tested
Numbers produced	6,426
Serial numbers	see W-4 listing
Chassis prefixes	IBH
Engine prefixes	IBHM
Chassis serial number location	pad on right side of crankcase
Engine serial number location	plate on left side of clutch housing

Regular Equipment
Information not available

Attachments and Special Features
Air pipe extension, belt pulley attachment, collector pre-cleaner, gasoline-distillate attachment, kerosene attachment, exhaust muffler, exhaust pipe extension, heavy-duty front axle with spring, front PTO, first and second front wheel weight sets, heat indicator for conventional radiator, heat indicator for pressurized radiator, hydraulic brakes, low-boiling-point thermostat and heat indicator for conventional radiator, 5,000- and 8,000-foot pistons for both gasoline and kerosene engines, rear PTO, radiator shutter, heavy-duty rear axle, first and second rear wheel weight sets, spark arrester, tire pump, Bosch "No Battery" lighting attachment, Delco-Remy lighting attachment, Delco-Remy starting attachment, Delco-Remy starting and lighting attachment, lighting attachment (tractors with starting attachment), reverse-flow radiator fan, side PTO, and a wide variety of wheel and tire options

Major Changes/Dates
I-4 production continued with Super W-4 features, but name was not changed
Discontinued May 14, 1953

Comments
Chassis and engine serial numbers may *not* match

International I-4 Heavy Duty

Engine	C-152
Cylinders	four
Bore and stroke	3 3/8x4 1/4 inches

Displacement ....152.1 cubic inches
Rated rpm 1,650
Compression ratio 5.9:1
Ignition..IH H-4 magneto
Carburetor..1-inch IH D-10 updraft
Cooling capacity ....4 1/4 gallons
Fuel tank capacity ....17 gallons
Horsepower ratings
    Drawbar...25
    PTO/belt 27.5
Length..121 inches
Wheelbase...71 3/4 inches
Height..62 3/4 inches
Width ....65 3/8 inches
Available treads ....52 1/4 inches (front), 46 1/8 inches
    (rear)
Weight ....4,400 pounds
Speed, forward,12.00x24 rear tires

Gear	Speed
1	2.2 mph
2	3.6 mph
3	5.2 mph
4	7.4 mph
5	15.5 mph
Reverse	3.0 mph

Price ....na
Nebraska test number....................................na
Numbers produced...na
Serial numbers ....see W-4 listing
Chassis prefixes ....IBH
Engine prefixes..IBHM
Chassis serial number location ....plate on left side of clutch housing
Engine serial number location........................pad on right side of crankcase

Regular Equipment

Heavy-duty front and rear axles and hydraulic rear brakes

Attachments and Special Features

Air pipe extension, belt pulley attachment, collector pre-cleaner, gasoline-distillate attachment, kerosene attachment, exhaust muffler, exhaust pipe extension, front PTO, first and second front wheel weight sets, heat indicator for conventional radiator, heat indicator for pressurized radiator, low-boiling-point thermostat and heat indicator for conventional radiator, 5,000- and 8,000-foot pistons for both gasoline and kerosene engines, rear PTO, radiator shutter, first and second rear wheel weight sets, spark arrester, tire pump, Bosch "No Battery" lighting attachment, Delco-Remy lighting attachment, Delco-Remy starting attachment, Delco-Remy starting and lighting attachment, lighting attachment (tractors with starting attachment), reverse-flow radiator fan, side PTO, and a wide variety of wheel and tire options

Major Changes/Dates

Information not available

Comments

Same as for I-4 except for heavy-duty front and rear axles and hydraulic brakes. However, they were sold as a complete package as such.

McCormick-Deering Super W-4

Engine C-164
Cylinders ....four
Bore and stroke..3 1/2x4 1/4 inches
Displacement ....164 cubic inches
Rated rpm 1,650
Compression ratio...6.1:1 gasoline, 4.64 distillate
Ignition...6-volt battery
Carburetor..1 1/4-inch IH updraft
Cooling capacity ....4 1/4 gallons
Fuel tank capacity ....17 gallons
Horsepower ratings
   Drawbar..29 gasoline, 26.5 distillate
   PTO/belt ....33 gasoline, 29.5 distillate
Length...114 inches
Wheelbase..66 5/8 inches
Height ....80 inches (at top of muffler)
Width ....66 5/8 inches
Available treads ....45 3/4 inches (front), 52 inches (rear)

SUPER W-4
The Super W-4 was an improved power W-4. It also received live hydraulics over the production run. State Historical Society of Wisconsin

Weight ....3,915 pounds without fuel or water
Speed
   Gear...*Speed*
   1 ....2.41 mph
   2 ....3.48 mph
   3 ....4.65 mph
   4 ....6.19 mph
   5 ....15.04 mph
   Reverse ....3.04 mph
Price ....na
Nebraska test number....................................491
Numbers produced
   1953..2,566 (includes some W-4 series)
   1954..444
   2,527 Super W-4s produced
Serial numbers
   1953..501–2667
   1954..2668–3292 (final serial number may
                       be 3932; sources conflict)
Chassis prefixes ....SWH
Engine prefixes...C-164
Chassis serial number location ....left side of clutch housing
Engine serial number location......................right side of engine above crankcase
                       breather

Regular Equipment
Information not available

Attachments and Special Features
Air intake and exhaust extensions, collector pre-cleaner, pre-screener, combination rear work and travel lamp, spark arrester, wheel weights, engine hour meter, high-altitude pistons, radiator shutter, hydraulic remote control, distillate or gasoline engine, belt pulley, swinging drawbar, muffler, PTO, deluxe upholstered seat pad, detachable seat pad, and pneumatic tire pump

Major Changes/Dates
Discontinued October 22, 1954

Comments
None

McCormick-Deering W-6
Engine...C-248
Cylinders ....four
Bore and stroke...3 7/8x5 1/4 inches
Displacement ....247.7 cubic inches
Rated rpm 1,450

Compression ratio..5.65:1
Ignition..IH H-4
Carburetor...1 1/4-inch IH E-12 updraft
Cooling capacity ....6 1/4 gallons
Fuel tank capacity ....21 gallons, 1 gallon starting
Horsepower ratings
    Drawbar..32.8
    PTO/belt...36.69
Length...124 3/8 inches
Wheelbase...76 inches
Height ....90 3/4 inches (at muffler)
Width ....63 inches
Available treads ....46 3/4 inches (front), 53 inches
    (rear)
Weight ....4,830 pounds (approximate ship-
    ping weight)

Speed

Gear	Speed
1	2 3/8 mph
2	3 1/8 mph
3	4 mph
4	4 7/8 mph
5	14 mph
Reverse	2 7/8 mph

Price $2,325 (1951)
Nebraska test number....................................355 and 354
Numbers produced (all -6 series)

Year	Number
1940	287
1941	2,558
1942	1,513
1943	1,180
1944	2,584
1945	3,273
1946	3,273
1947	5,322
1948	5,251
1949	5,498
1950	4,735
1951	5,875
1952	3,838 (includes some Super W-6s)
1953	6,627 (includes some Super W-6s)

28,378 W-6s produced

Serial numbers

Year	Serial numbers
1940	501–1224
1941	1225–3717
1942	3718–5056
1943	5057–6312 or 6311

1944	6313–9495 or 6312–9393
1945	9496–14152 or 9394–14017
1946	14153–17791 or 14018–16810
1947	17792–22980 or 16811–22981
1948	22981–28703 or 22982–28705
1949	28704–33697 or 28706–33697
1950	33698–38517
1951	38518–44317
1952	44318–45273
1953	45274–46011
1954	na
Chassis prefixes	WBK
Engine prefixes	WBKM
Chassis serial number location	left side of clutch housing
Engine serial number location	pad on right side of crankcase

Regular Equipment

Gasoline engine, pneumatic tires, magneto, heat indicator, front drawbar, adjustable flat-bar-type drawbar, and tilt-back waterproof upholstered seat (adjustable forward and back)

Attachments and Special Features

Steel wheels with spade lugs, distillate-gasoline engines with radiator shutters, engine-operated tire pump, PTO, electric starting and lighting, swinging drawbar, exhaust muffler, spark arrester, pre-cleaner, wheel weights, and 5,000- and 8,000-foot high-altitude pistons

Major Changes/Dates

First W-6 (WBK 501) built May 6, 1940
Discontinued March 27, 1952

Comments

None

McCormick-Deering WD-6

Engine	D-248
Cylinders	four
Bore and stroke	3 7/8x5 1/4 inches
Displacement	247.7 cubic inches
Rated rpm	1,450
Compression ratio	14.2:1
Ignition	IH H-4
Carburetor	IH F-8
Cooling capacity	7 gallons
Fuel tank capacity	21 gallons, 1 gallon starting

Horsepower ratings
    Drawbar..31.38 (IH)
    PTO/belt ....36.38 (IH)
Length..124 3/8 inches
Wheelbase..76 inches
Height ....89 1/4 inches (at top of muffler)
Width ....63 inches
Available treads ....53 inches (drive wheels), 46 3/4 inches (front)
Weight ....5,250 pounds (approximate shipping weight)

Speed
    Gear...*Speed*
    1 ....2 3/8 mph
    2 ....3 1/8 mph
    3 ....4 mph
    4 ....4 7/8 mph
    5 ....14 mph
    Reverse ....2 7/8 mph
Price $3,124 (1951)
Nebraska test number...................................356 and 459
Numbers produced.......................................na
Serial numbers ....see W-6 listing
Chassis prefixes ....WDBK
Engine prefixes...WDBKM
Chassis serial number location ....left side of clutch housing
Engine serial number location......................top milled section of left crankcase

Regular Equipment
    Diesel engine, pneumatic tires, magneto, heat indicator, front drawbar, adjustable flat-bar-type drawbar, and tilt-back waterproof upholstered seat (adjustable forward and back)

Attachments and Special Features
    Steel wheels with spade lugs, radiator shutters, engine-operated tire pump, PTO, electric starting and lighting, swinging drawbar, exhaust muffler, spark arrester, pre-cleaner, and wheel weights

Major Changes/Dates
    Discontinued March 27, 1952

Comments
    None

McCormick-Deering O-6
Engine C-248
Cylinders ....four

0-6

The O-6 featured full-wheel fenders and shields, as well as the rerouted exhaust. Today, it is a very rare and beautiful tractor and hard to find in good shape. In their day, these tractors took a lot of abuse from tree branches—this one's grille has already been abused. *State Historical Society of Wisconsin*

Bore and stroke	3 7/8x5 1/4 inches
Displacement	247.7 cubic inches
Rated rpm	950–1,450
Compression ratio	5.9:1
Ignition	IH H-4
Carburetor	1 1/4-inch IH E-12 updraft
Cooling capacity	6 gallons
Fuel tank capacity	21 gallons, 1 gallon starting
Horsepower ratings	
Drawbar	32 distillate, 33.5 gasoline (IH)
PTO/belt	36 distillate, 38.5 gasoline (IH)
Length	133 1/4 inches
Wheelbase	76 1/4 inches
Height	61 1/2 inches (at steering wheel), 63 inches with steering cowl
Width	65 inches
Available treads	46 3/4 inches (front), 45 inches (rear)
Weight	5,435 pounds (equipped shipping weight)

Speed

Gear	Speed
1	1 mph
2	3 1/8 mph
3	4 1/8 mph
4	4 7/8 mph
5	14 5/8 mph
Reverse	1 7/8 mph

Price $2,460 (1951)
Nebraska test number....................................na
Numbers produced..1,962
Serial numbers ....see W-6 listing
Chassis prefixes ....OBK
Engine prefixes ....OBKM
Chassis serial number location ....left side of clutch housing
Engine serial number location......................pad on right side of crankcase

Regular Equipment

Gasoline engine, heat indicator, magneto, hand-operated single-plate over-center clutch, front drawbar, low-swinging adjustable drawbar, tilt-back waterproof upholstered seat, and pneumatic tires

Attachments and Special Features

Distillate engine, radiator shutter, belt pulleys, PTO, electric starting and lighting, wheel weights, steering wheel cowl, 7-mph 4th gear, engine-operated tire pump, 5,000- and 8,000-foot high-altitude pistons, and steering wheel cowl

Major Changes/Dates

First kerosene-distillate O-6 (OBK 811, engine OBKM-501) built November 27, 1940
Discontinued November 1, 1952

Comments

None

McCormick-Deering OS-6

Engine C-248
Cylinders ....four
Bore and stroke ....3 7/8x5 1/4 inches
Displacement ....247.7 cubic inches

OS-6
The OS-6 only had some of the O-6 features, such as the rerouted exhaust and low seat. It is a very rare tractor, although not quite as desirable as the "Buck Rogers" O-6. *State Historical Society of Wisconsin*

Rated rpm 950–1,450
Compression ratio..14.2:1
Ignition..IH H-4
Carburetor..1 1/4-inch IH E-12 updraft
Cooling capacity ....6 1/4 gallons
Fuel tank capacity ....21 gallons, 7/8 gallon starting
Horsepower ratings
    Drawbar..32 distillate, 33.5 gasoline
    PTO/belt ....36 distillate, 38.5 gasoline
Length...133 1/4 inches
Wheelbase...76 1/4 inches
Height ....61 inches (at steering wheel)
Width ....59 3/4 inches
Available treads ....46 3/4 inches (front), 45 inches (rear)
Weight ....5,120 equipped pounds
Speed
    Gear..*Speed*
    1 ....1 mph
    2 ....3 1/8 mph
    3 ....4 1/8 mph
    4 ....4 7/8 mph
    5 ....14 5/8 mph
    Reverse ....1 7/8 mph
Price $2,335 (1951)
Nebraska test number.....................................na
Numbers produced..831
Serial numbers ....see W-6 listing
Chassis prefixes ....OBKS
Engine prefixes...OBKSM
Chassis serial number location ....left side of clutch housing
Engine serial number location......................pad on right side of crankcase

Regular Equipment
    Gasoline engine, heat indicator, magneto, hand-operated single-plate over-center clutch, front drawbar, low-swinging adjustable drawbar, tilt-back waterproof upholstered seat, and pneumatic tires

Attachments and Special Features
    Distillate engine, radiator shutter, belt pulleys, PTO, electric starting and lighting, wheel weights, steering wheel cowl, 7-mph 4th gear, engine-operated tire pump, and 5,000- and 8,000-foot high-altitude pistons

Major Changes/Dates
    Model OS-6 production authorized October 19, 1944, probably not produced until November 30, 1944
    Discontinued November 1, 1952

Comments
    None

McCormick-Deering ODS-6

Engine	D-248
Cylinders	four
Bore and stroke	3 7/8x5 1/4 inches
Displacement	247.7 cubic inches
Rated rpm	800–1,450
Compression ratio	14.2:1
Ignition	IH H-4
Carburetor	IH F-8
Cooling capacity	6 3/4 gallons
Fuel tank capacity	20 1/2 gallons, 7/8 gallon starting

Horsepower ratings

Drawbar	31.5 (IH)
PTO/belt	36 (IH)
Length	133 1/4 inches
Wheelbase	76 1/4 inches
Height	61 inches
Width	59 3/4 inches
Available treads	46 3/4 inches (front), 45 inches (rear)
Weight	5,540 pounds

Speed, forward, 13.00x26 tires

Gear	Speed
1	1 mph
2	3 1/8 mph
3	4 1/8 mph
4	4 7/8 mph
5	14 5/8 mph
Reverse	1 7/8 mph

Price	na
Nebraska test number	na
Numbers produced	352
Serial numbers	see W-6 listing
Chassis prefixes	ODBKS
Engine prefixes	ODBKSM
Chassis serial number location	left side of clutch housing
Engine serial number location	top milled section of left crankcase

Regular Equipment
    Diesel engine, heat indicator, magneto, hand-operated single-plate over-center clutch, front drawbar, low-swinging adjustable drawbar, tilt-back waterproof upholstered seat, and pneumatic tires

Attachments and Special Features
Radiator shutter, belt pulleys, PTO, electric starting and lighting, wheel weights, steering wheel cowl, 7-mph 4th gear, and engine-operated tire pump

Major Changes/Dates
Information not available

Comments
None

International I-6

Engine	C-248
Cylinders	four
Bore and stroke	3 7/8x5 1/4 inches
Displacement	247.7 cubic inches
Rated rpm	1,450
Compression ratio	14.2:1
Ignition	IH H-4
Carburetor	1 1/4-inch IH E-12 updraft
Cooling capacity	6 1/4 gallons
Fuel tank capacity	21 gallons
Horsepower ratings	
Drawbar	34
PTO/belt	38.5
Length	125 1/4 inches
Wheelbase	76 1/4 inches
Height	68 3/4 inches
Width	64 inches
Available treads	46 3/4 inches (front), 50 inches (rear)
Weight	4,840 pounds
Speed	
Gear	*Speed*
1	2.2 mph
2	3.6 mph
3	5.3 mph
4	7.4 mph
5	14.3 mph
Reverse	2.6 mph
Price	na
Nebraska test number	na
Numbers produced	na
Serial numbers	see W-6 listing
Chassis prefixes	IBK
Engine prefixes	IBKM
Chassis serial number location	plate on left side of clutch housing
Engine serial number location	pad on right side of crankcase

Regular Equipment
Information not available

Attachments and Special Features
Air pipe extension, belt pulley attachment, collector pre-cleaner, gasoline-distillate attachment, kerosene attachment, exhaust muffler, exhaust pipe extension, heavy-duty front axle with spring, front PTO, first and second front wheel weight sets, heat indicator for conventional radiator, heat indicator for pressurized radiator, hour meter, hydraulic brakes, low-boiling-point thermostat and heat indicator for conventional radiator, rear PTO, radiator shutter, heavy-duty rear axle, first and second rear wheel weight sets, spark arrester, 5,000- and 8,000-foot pistons for both gasoline and kerosene engines, tire pump, Bosch "No Battery" lighting attachment, Delco-Remy lighting attachment, Delco-Remy starting attachment, Delco-Remy starting and lighting attachment, lighting attachment (tractors with starting attachment), reverse-flow radiator fan, side PTO, and a wide variety of wheel and tire options

Major Changes/Dates
Discontinued November 1, 1952

Comments
None

International I-6 Heavy Duty

Engine C-248
Cylinders ....four
Bore and stroke ....3 7/8x5 1/4 inches
Displacement ....247.7 cubic inches
Rated rpm 1,450
Compression ratio 5.65:1
Ignition...IH H-4
Carburetor...1 1/4-inch IH E-12 updraft
Cooling capacity ....6 1/4 gallons
Fuel tank capacity ....21 gallons
Horsepower ratings
    Drawbar...34
    PTO/belt 38.5
Length..130 5/8 inches
Wheelbase...82 5/8 inches
Height ....67 3/4 inches
Width ....65 3/8 inches
Available treads ....52 1/4 inches (front), 50 1/8 inches
          (rear)
Weight ....5,470 pounds
Speed
   Gear..Speed
   1 ....2.2 mph

2	3.6 mph
3	5.3 mph
4	7.4 mph
5	14.3 mph
Reverse	2.6 mph
Price	na
Nebraska test number	na
Numbers produced	na
Serial numbers	see W-6 listing
Chassis prefixes	IBK
Engine prefixes	IBKM
Chassis serial number location	plate on left side of clutch housing
Engine serial number location	pad on right side of crankcase

Regular Equipment
Information not available

Attachments and Special Features
Air pipe extension, belt pulley attachment, collector pre-cleaner, gasoline-distillate attachment, kerosene attachment, 5,000- and 8,000-foot pistons for both gasoline and kerosene engines, exhaust muffler, exhaust pipe extension, front PTO, first and second front wheel weight sets, heat indicator for conventional radiator, heat indicator for pressurized radiator, hour meter, low-boiling-point thermostat and heat indicator for conventional radiator, rear PTO, radiator shutter, first and second rear wheel weight sets, spark arrester, tire pump, Bosch "No Battery" lighting attachment, Delco-Remy lighting attachment, Delco-Remy starting attachment, Delco-Remy starting and lighting attachment, lighting attachment (tractors with starting attachment), reverse-flow radiator fan, side PTO, and a wide variety of wheel and tire options

Major Changes/Dates
Information not available

Comments
Same as I-6 except for heavy-duty front and rear axles and hydraulic brakes. However, they were sold as a complete package as such.

International ID-6

Engine	D-248
Cylinders	four
Bore and stroke	3 7/8x5 1/4 inches
Displacement	247.7 cubic inches
Rated rpm	1,450
Compression ratio	14.2:1
Ignition	IH H-4
Carburetor	IH F-8

Cooling capacity ....6 3/4 gallons
Fuel tank capacity ....20 gallons
Horsepower ratings
    Drawbar..32
    PTO/belt 36
Length...125 1/4 inches
Wheelbase...76 1/4 inches
Height ....68 3/4 inches
Width ....64 inches
Available treads ....46 3/4 inches (front), 50 inches (rear)
Weight ....5,175 pounds
Speed
    Gear ....*Speed*
    1 ....2.2 mph
    2 ....3.6 mph
    3 ....5.3 mph
    4 ....7.4 mph
    5 ....14.3 mph
    Reverse ....2.6 mph
Price ....na
Nebraska test number....................................na
Numbers produced...na
Serial numbers ....see W-6 listing
Chassis prefixes ....IDBK
Engine prefixes...IDBKM
Chassis serial number location ....plate on left side of clutch housing
Engine serial number location.......................top milled section of left crankcase

Regular Equipment
    Information not available

Attachments and Special Features
    Air pipe extension, belt pulley attachment, collector pre-cleaner, exhaust muffler, exhaust pipe extension, heavy-duty front axle with spring, front PTO, first and second front wheel weight sets, heat indicator for conventional radiator, heat indicator for pressurized radiator, hour meter, hydraulic brakes, low-boiling-point thermostat and heat indicator for conventional radiator, rear PTO, radiator shutter, heavy-duty rear axle, first and second rear wheel weight sets, spark arrester, tire pump, Bosch "No Battery" lighting attachment, Delco-Remy lighting attachment, Delco-Remy starting attachment, Delco-Remy starting and lighting attachment, lighting attachment (tractors with starting attachment), reverse-flow radiator fan, side PTO, and a wide variety of wheel and tire options

Major Changes/Dates
    Information not available

Comments
    None

International ID-6 Heavy Duty

Engine..D-248
Cylinders ....four
Bore and stroke...3 7/8x5 1/4 inches
Displacement ....247.7 cubic inches
Rated rpm 1,450
Compression ratio..14.2:1
Ignition...IH H-4
Carburetor..IH F-8
Cooling capacity ....6 3/4 gallons
Fuel tank capacity ....20 gallons
Horsepower ratings
    Drawbar..32
    PTO/belt 36
Length..130 5/8 inches
Wheelbase..82 5/8 inches
Height ....67 3/4 inches
Width ....65 3/8 inches
Available treads ....52 1/4 inches (front), 50 1/8 inches
                                                                     (rear)
Weight ....5,875 pounds
Speed

Gear	Speed
1	2.2 mph
2	3.6 mph
3	5.3 mph
4	7.4 mph
5	14.3 mph
Reverse	2.6 mph

Price ....na
Nebraska test number....................................na
Numbers produced...na
Serial numbers ....see W-6 listing
Chassis prefixes ....IDBK
Engine prefixes..IDBKM
Chassis serial number location ....top milled section of left crankcase
Engine serial number location.......................plate on left side of clutch housing

Regular Equipment
    Information not available

Attachments and Special Features
    Acetylene headlight, engine side curtains, special-size pulleys, extensions for rear and front wheels, variety of lugs, special low-drawbar

acetylene headlight, special-size pulleys, extensions for rear and front wheels, variety of lugs, special low-drawbar air-pipe extension, belt pulley attachment, collector pre-cleaner, exhaust muffler, exhaust pipe extension, front PTO, first and second front wheel weight sets, heat indicator for conventional radiator, heat indicator for pressurized radiator, hour meter, low-boiling-point thermostat and heat indicator for conventional radiator, 5,000- and 8,000-foot pistons for both gasoline and kerosene engines, rear PTO, radiator shutter, first and second rear wheel weight sets, spark arrester, tire pump, Bosch "No Battery" lighting attachment, Delco-Remy lighting attachment, Delco-Remy starting attachment, Delco-Remy starting and lighting attachment, lighting attachment (tractors with starting attachment), reverse-flow radiator fan, side PTO, and a wide variety of wheel and tire options

Major Changes/Dates

Information not available

Comments

Same as ID-6 except for heavy-duty front and rear axles and hydraulic brakes. However, they were sold as a complete package as such.

McCormick-Deering Super W-6

Engine C-264
Cylinders ....four
Bore and stroke ....4x5 1/4 inches
Displacement ....264 cubic inches
Rated rpm 1,450
Compression ratio 5.9:1
Ignition...6-volt battery
Carburetor..1 1/4-inch IH E-12 updraft

SUPER W-6
The Super W-6 was intended for wide-open, small-grain fields that didn't require a row-crop tractor. The Super W-6 was an improved power version of the W-6 and got live hydraulics and a channel frame similar to the M's. *State Historical Society of Wisconsin*

147

Cooling capacity ....6 gallons
Fuel tank capacity ....21 gallons, 7/8 gallon starting
Horsepower ratings
    Drawbar..42 gasoline, 36 distillate
    PTO/belt ....47.5 gasoline, 41 distillate
Length...125 inches
Wheelbase...75 7/8 inches
Height ....90 7/8 inches
Width ....70 inches
Available treads ....55 inches (rear), 46 5/8 inches (front)
Weight ....5,070 pounds with regular equipment
Speed
    Gear..*Speed*
    1 ....2 5/8 mph
    2 ....3 5/8 mph
    3 ....4 3/4 mph
    4 ....6 5/8 mph
    5 ....16 1/8 mph
    Reverse ....3 mph
Price ....na
Nebraska test number....................................476 and 485 (LPG)
Numbers produced
    1952...3,838 (includes some W-6s)
    1953...6,627 (includes some W-6s)
    1954...3,089
    6,891 Super W-6s produced
Serial numbers
    1952...501–2907 or 501–2276
    1953...2908–8996 or 2277–8996
    1954...8997–9084
Chassis prefixes SW-6
Engine prefixes...C-264
Chassis serial number location ....plate on left side of clutch housing
Engine serial number location.......................right side of crankcase above ignition unit

Regular Equipment

Gasoline engine with battery ignition, starter and lights, fenders, deluxe foam rubber seat, belt pulley, PTO, swinging drawbar, muffler, and heat indicator

Attachments and Special Features

Distillate engine, LPG engine and equipment, magneto ignition, jute seat, hydraulic remote control, radiator shutter, hour meter, high-altitude pistons, wheel weights, dual rear lamp, spark arrester, intake extension, exhaust extension, collector pre-cleaner, and pre-screener

Major Changes/Dates
Discontinued February 8, 1954

Comments
None

McCormick-Deering Super WD-6

Engine D-264
Cylinders ....four
Bore and stroke ....4x5 1/4 inches
Displacement ....264 cubic inches
Rated rpm 1,450
Compression ratio 16.5:1
Ignition...12-volt battery
Carburetor..IH F-8
Cooling capacity ....7 gallons
Fuel tank capacity ....20 1/2 gallons, 7/8 gallon starting
Horsepower ratings
    Drawbar...42 (IH)
    PTO/belt ....47.5 (IH)
Length..125 inches
Wheelbase..75 7/8 inches
Height...89 3/8 inches (at top of muffler)
Width ....70 inches
Available treads ....55 inches (rear), 46 5/8 inches (front)
Weight ....5,490 pounds with regular equip-
    ment

Speed

Gear	Speed
1	2 5/8 mph
2	3 5/8 mph
3	4 3/4 mph
4	6 5/8 mph
5	16 1/8 mph
Reverse	3 mph

Price ....na
Nebraska test number....................................478
Numbers produced..1,691
Serial numbers ....see Super W-6 listing
Chassis prefixes SWD-6
Engine prefixes...D-264
Chassis serial number location ....plate on left side of clutch housing
Engine serial number location.......................left side of crankcase above injection
    pump

Regular Equipment
Diesel engine with battery ignition for starting, starter and lights,

fenders, deluxe foam rubber seat, belt pulley, PTO, swinging drawbar, muffler, and heat indicator

Attachments and Special Features
Magneto ignition, jute seat, hydraulic remote control, radiator shutter, hour meter, wheel weights, dual rear lamp, spark arrester, intake extension, exhaust extension, collector pre-cleaner, and pre-screener

Major Changes/Dates
Discontinued February 25, 1954
Comments
None

McCormick-Deering Super W-6-TA

Engine C-264
Cylinders ....four
Bore and stroke ....4x5 1/4 inches
Displacement ....264 cubic inches
Rated rpm 1,450
Compression ratio ....na
Ignition..na
Carburetor..na
Cooling capacity ....6 gallons
Fuel tank capacity ....21 gallons
Horsepower ratings
   Drawbar...43.71 (IH)
   PTO/belt..48.77 (IH)
Length..130 inches
Wheelbase..81 inches
Height...93 3/8 inches (at top of muffler)
Width ....70 inches
Available treads ....50 3/4 inches (front), 55 inches (rear)
Weight ....5,400 pounds (no fluids)
Speed

Gear	Speed regular	TA
1	2 3/8 mph	1 5/8 mph
2	3 3/4 mph	2 mph
3	4 5/8 mph	3 1/8 mph
4	6 mph	4 3/8 mph
5	16 1/8 mph	10 7/8 mph
Reverse	3 1/4 mph	2 1/8 mph

Price ....na
Nebraska test number.....................................na
Numbers produced..3,089 (1954)
Serial numbers 10001–13006 (1954)
Chassis prefixes SW6-TA

Engine prefixes...C-264
Chassis serial number location ....left side of clutch housing
Engine serial number location........................right side of engine above crankcase
breather

Regular Equipment
Lights and TA

Attachments and Special Features
Information not available

Major Changes/Dates
Discontinued November 15, 1954

Comments
None

McCormick-Deering Super W-6-TA Diesel
Engine D-264
Cylinders ....four
Bore and stroke...4x5 1/4 inches
Displacement ....264 cubic inches
Rated rpm 900–1,450
Compression ratio...16.5:1
Ignition..na
Carburetor...na
Cooling capacity ....7 gallons
Fuel tank capacity ....20 gallons
Horsepower ratings
    Drawbar..43.77 (IH)
    PTO/belt ....48.47 (IH)
Length...130 inches
Wheelbase...81 inches
Height ....91 3/4 inches (at top of muffler)
Width ....70 inches
Available treads ....55 inches (rear), 50 3/4 inches
(front)
Weight ....5,815 pounds
Speed

Gear	Speed	
	regular	with TA
1	2 3/8 mph	1 5/8 mph
2	3 3/4 mph	2 mph
3	4 5/8 mph	3 1/8 mph
4	6 mph	4 3/8 mph
5	16 1/8 mph	10 7/8 mph
Reverse	3 1/4 mph	2 1/8 mph

Price ....na
Nebraska test number....................................na
Numbers produced..na
Serial numbers ....see Super W-6-TA listing
Chassis prefixes ....na
Engine prefixes...D-264
Chassis serial number location ....plate on left side of clutch housing
Engine serial number location.......................na

Regular Equipment
   Information not available

Attachments and Special Features
   Information not available

Major Changes/Dates
   Discontinued January 10, 1955

Comments
   None

McCormick-Deering W-9

Engine C-335
Cylinders ....four
Bore and stroke ....4.4x5.5 inches
Displacement ....335 cubic inches
Rated rpm 1,500
Compression ratio...........................5.4:1
Ignition...IH H-4
Carburetor......................................1 3/8-inch IH E-13 updraft
Cooling capacity ....10 gallons
Fuel tank capacity ....36 gallons
Horsepower ratings
   Drawbar....................................44.59 distillate, 47.06 gasoline (IH)
   PTO/belt ....49 distillate, 52.36 gasoline (IH)
Length...134 1/4 inches
Wheelbase......................................83 3/8 inches
Height ....83 inches
Width ....75 3/4 inches
Available treads ....60 inches (rear), 52 inches (front)
Weight ....5,600 pounds
Speed, forward, 14.00x34 tires
   Gear...*Speed*
   1 ....2 3/8 mph
   2 ....3 1/8 mph
   3 ....4 mph
   4 ....5 mph

5	15 3/4 mph
Reverse	2 7/8 mph
Price	$3,162 (1951)
Nebraska test number	369 and 371

Numbers produced

1940	na
1941	1,764
1942	1,263
1943	1,220
1944	5,765
1945	5,868
1946	5,373
1947	6,235
1948	6,247
1949	9,485
1950	6,937
1951	7,231
1952	5,815
1953	4,773
1954	3,662

Serial numbers

1940	501–577
1941	578–2992 or 578–3002
1942	2993–3650 or 3003–3650
1943	3651–5393 or 3651–5500
1944	5394–11458 or 5501–11458
1945	11459–17288 or 11459–17293
1946	17289–22713 or 17294–22714
1947	22714–29206 or 22715–29206
1948	29207–36158
1949	36159–45550 or 36159–45549
1950	45551–51738 or 45550–51738
1951	51739–59406
1952	59407–64013
1953	64014–67919 or 64014–69968
1954	67969–up
Chassis prefixes	WCB

NINE SERIES SERIAL NUMBER LOCATION

The Nine Series tractors have the serial number plate mounted on the right side of the fuel tank support, located above the clutch housing. It can be seen here to the right of and above the two hoses and to the left of the filter.

Engine prefixes...WCBM
Chassis serial number location ....nameplate on fuel tank support
Engine serial number location........................right side of engine crankcase

Regular Equipment

Gasoline engine, pneumatic tires, magneto, heat indicator, front drawbar, adjustable flat-bar-type drawbar, and tilt-back waterproof upholstered seat (adjustable forward and back)

Attachments and Special Features

Distillate engine, magneto ignition, jute seat, hydraulic remote control, radiator shutter, low-temp thermostat, hour meter, variable-tread rear rims, high-altitude pistons, wheel weights, dual rear lamp, spark arrester, intake extension, exhaust extension, collector pre-cleaner, and pre-screener

Major Changes/Dates

New standard PTO attachment and redesigned rear platform (60790-DA replaced 60790-D) on tractor WCB 14401, produced on or before August 18, 1945

New crankcase 8318 DCXA (replaced 8318 DCX) on engine WCBM 16587, produced September 27, 1946

Comments

None

McCormick-Deering WD-9

Engine D-335
Cylinders ....four
Bore and stroke..4.4x5.5 inches
Displacement ....335 cubic inches
Rated rpm 1,500
Compression ratio...15.7:1
Ignition..IH H-4
Carburetor..IH Model F-8
Cooling capacity ....11 gallons
Fuel tank capacity ....35 gallons, 7/8 gallon starting
Horsepower ratings
   Drawbar...48.45 (IH)
   PTO/belt ....53.24 (IH)
Length...134 1/4 inches
Wheelbase..83 inches
Height..81 7/8 inches (at top of muffler)
Width ....75 3/4 inches
Available treads ....60 inches (rear), 52 inches (front)
Weight ....5,850 pounds

peed, forward, 14.00x34 tires

Gear	Speed
1	2 3/8 mph
2	3 1/8 mph
3	4 mph
4	5 mph
5	15 3/4 mph
Reverse	2 7/8 mph

rice 3,845 (1951)
Jebraska test number .... 370 and 441
Jumbers produced .... na
erial numbers .... see W-9 listing
Chassis prefixes .... WDCB
ngine prefixes .... WDCBM
Chassis serial number location .... nameplate on fuel tank support
ngine serial number location .... top milled section on left side of
engine crankcase

Regular Equipment
Diesel engine, pneumatic tires, magneto, heat indicator, front drawbar, adjustable flat-bar-type drawbar, and tilt-back waterproof upholstered seat (adjustable forward and back)

Attachments and Special Features
Magneto ignition, jute seat, hydraulic remote control, radiator shutter, low-temp thermostat, hour meter, variable-tread rear rims, wheel weights, dual rear lamp, spark arrester, intake extension, exhaust extension, and collector pre-cleaner

Major Changes/Dates
First tractor (WDCB 501) produced December 4, 1940
New standard PTO attachment and redesigned rear platform (60790-DA replaced 60790-D) on tractor WDCB 14822, produced on or before August 18, 1945
New crankcase 8124-DHXA (replaced 8124-DHX) on engine WDCBM 5870, produced October 1, 1946

Comments
None

International I-9
ngine C-335
Cylinders .... four
Bore and stroke .... 4.4x5.5 inches
Displacement .... 334.5 cubic inches
Rated rpm 1,500
Compression ratio 5.4:1

Ignition..IH H-4
Carburetor...1 3/8-inch IH E-13 updraft
Cooling capacity ....10 gallons
Fuel tank capacity ....36 gallons
Horsepower ratings
    Drawbar..46.5
    PTO/belt 52
Length...132 1/4 inches
Wheelbase...83 5/8 inches
Height ....88 inches
Width ....67 3/4 inches
Available treads ....52 inches (front), 50 inches (rear)
Weight ....6,395 pounds
Speed
    Gear..*Speed*
    1 ....2.3 mph
    2 ....3.1 mph
    3 ....5.3 mph
    4 ....7.3 mph
    5 ....15.2 mph
    Reverse ....2.8 mph
Price ....na
Nebraska test number.....................................na
Numbers produced...na
Serial numbers ....see W-9 listing
Chassis prefixes ....ICB
Engine prefixes...ICBM
Chassis serial number location ....nameplate on fuel tank support
Engine serial number location.......................right side of engine crankcase

Regular Equipment
    Information not available

Attachments and Special Features
    Air pipe extension, belt pulley attachment, collector pre-cleaner, gasoline-distillate attachment, kerosene attachment, exhaust muffler, exhaust pipe extension, heavy-duty front axle with spring, front PTO, first and second front wheel weight sets, heat indicator for conventional radiator, heat indicator for pressurized radiator, hour meter, hydraulic brakes, low-boiling-point thermostat and heat indicator for conventional radiator, 5,000- and 8,000-foot pistons for both gasoline and kerosene engines, rear PTO, radiator shutter, heavy-duty rear axle, first and second rear wheel weight sets, spark arrester, tire pump, Bosch "No Battery" lighting attachment, Delco-Remy lighting attachment, Delco-Remy starting attachment, Delco-Remy starting and lighting attachment, lighting attachment (tractors with starting attachment), side PTO, and a wide variety of wheel and tire options

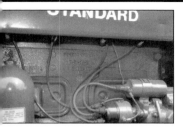

NINE SERIES SERIAL NUMBER LOCATION
On this Nine Series tractor, the engine serial number plate is much more visible behind the ignition unit, which is clearly visible over the top of the coil.

Major Changes/Dates
New crankcase 8318 DCXA (replaced 8318 DCX) on engine ICBM 6610, produced September 30, 1946

Comments
None

International I-9 Heavy Duty

Engine	C-335
Cylinders	four
Bore and stroke	4.4x5 inches
Displacement	334.5 cubic inches
Rated rpm	1,500
Compression ratio	5.4:1
Ignition	IH H-4
Carburetor	1 3/8-inch IH E-13 updraft
Cooling capacity	10 gallons
Fuel tank capacity	36 gallons

Horsepower ratings

Drawbar	46.5
PTO/belt	52
Length	138 inches
Wheelbase	87 7/8 inches
Height	88 inches
Width	67 7/8 inches
Available treads	51 inches (front), 50 inches (rear)
Weight	7,240 pounds

Speed

Gear	Speed
1	2.3 mph
2	3.1 mph
3	5.3 mph
4	7.3 mph
5	15.2 mph
Reverse	2.8 mph
Price	na
Nebraska test number	na

Numbers produced...na
Serial numbers ....see W-9 listing
Chassis prefixes ....ICB
Engine prefixes..ICBM
Chassis serial number location ....nameplate on fuel tank support
Engine serial number location.......................right side of engine crankcase

Regular Equipment
Information not available

Attachments and Special Features
Air pipe extension, belt pulley attachment, collector pre-cleaner, gaso line-distillate attachment, kerosene attachment, exhaust muffler, exhaust pipe extension, front PTO, first and second front wheel weight sets, heat indicator for conventional radiator, heat indicator for pressurized radiator, hour meter, low-boiling-point thermostat and heat indicator for conventional radiator, 5,000- and 8,000-foot pistons for both gasoline and kerosene engines, rear PTO, radiator shutter, first and second rear wheel weight sets, spark arrester, tire pump, Bosch "No Battery" lighting attachment, Delco-Remy lighting attachment, Delco-Remy starting attachment, Delco-Remy starting and lighting attachment, lighting attachment (tractors with starting attachment), side PTO, and a wide variety of wheel and tire options

Major Changes/Dates
Information not available

Comments
Same as Model I-9 except for heavy-duty front and rear axles and hydraulic brakes. However, they were sold as a complete package as such.

International ID-9 Heavy Duty
Engine..D-335
Cylinders ....four
Bore and stroke...4.4x5 inches
Displacement ....334.5 cubic inches
Rated rpm 1,500
Compression ratio...15.7:1
Ignition..IH H-4
Carburetor...IH F-8
Cooling capacity ....11 gallons
Fuel tank capacity ....35 gallons
Horsepower ratings
   Drawbar...44
   PTO/belt...49
Length..138 inches
Wheelbase...87 7/8 inches
Height ....88 inches

Width ....67 7/8 inches
Available treads ....51 inches (front), 50 inches (rear)
Weight ....7,595 pounds
Speed

Gear	*Speed*
1	2.3 mph
2	3.1 mph
3	5.3 mph
4	7.3 mph
5	15.2 mph
Reverse	2.8 mph

Price ....na
Nebraska test number....................................na
Numbers produced...na
Serial numbers ....see W-9 listing
Chassis prefixes ....IDCB
Engine prefixes...IDCBM
Chassis serial number location ....nameplate on fuel tank support
Engine serial number location.......................top milled section on left side of
engine crankcase

Regular Equipment

Heavy-duty front and rear axles

Attachments and Special Features

Air pipe extension, belt pulley attachment, collector pre-cleaner, exhaust muffler, exhaust pipe extension, front PTO, first and second front wheel weight sets, heat indicator for conventional radiator, heat indicator for pressurized radiator, hour meter, low-boiling-point thermostat and heat indicator for conventional radiator, rear PTO, radiator shutter, first and second rear wheel weight sets, spark arrester, tire pump, Bosch "No Battery" lighting attachment, Delco-Remy lighting attachment, Delco-Remy starting attachment, Delco-Remy starting and lighting attachment, lighting attachment (tractors with starting attachment), side PTO, and a wide variety of wheel and tire options

Major Changes/Dates

Information not available

Comments

Same as Model ID-9 except for heavy-duty front and rear axles and hydraulic brakes. However, they were sold as a complete package as such.

International ID-9

Engine..D-335
Cylinders ....four
Bore and stroke..4.4x5.5 inches

Displacement ....334.5 cubic inches
Rated rpm 1,500
Compression ratio ....na
Ignition...IH H-4
Carburetor..IH F-8
Cooling capacity ....11 gallons
Fuel tank capacity ....36 gallons, 1 gallon starting
Horsepower ratings..na
Length...131 7/8 inches
Wheelbase..83 3/8 inches
Height ....68 5/8 inches
Width ....66 3/4 inches
Available treads ....52 inches (front), 50 inches (rear)
Weight ....6,400 pounds (approximate ship-
ping weight)

Speed

Gear	Speed
1	2.3 mph
2	3.1 mph
3	5.2 mph
4	7.3 mph
5	15.1 mph
Reverse	2.8 mph

Price ....na
Nebraska test number....................................na
Numbers produced...na
Serial numbers ....see W-9 listing
Chassis prefixes ....IDCB
Engine prefixes...IDCBM
Chassis serial number location ....nameplate on fuel tank support
Engine serial number location.........................top milled section on left side of
engine crankcase

Regular Equipment
Information not available

Attachments and Special Features
Air pipe extension, belt pulley attachment, collector pre-cleaner, exhaust muffler, exhaust pipe extension, heavy-duty front axle with spring, front PTO, first and second front wheel weight sets, heat indicator for conventional radiator, heat indicator for pressurized radiator, hour meter, hydraulic brakes, low-boiling-point thermostat and heat indicator for conventional radiator, rear PTO, radiator shutter, heavy-duty rear axle, first and second rear wheel weight sets, spark arrester, tire pump, Bosch "No Battery" lighting attachment, Delco-Remy lighting attachment, Delco-Remy starting attachment, Delco-Remy starting and lighting attachment, lighting attachment (tractors with starting attachment),

Super WDR-9s
These Super WDR-9s were intended for the tough demands of rice farming, with foot decelerators for crossing levees and the squared-off rear-wheel fenders shown here. They are powerful and well-equipped but aren't very common today. Other rice tractors, such as the WDR-9, WR-9, and WR-9S, had similar fenders.
State Historical Society of Wisconsin

side PTO, and a wide variety of wheel and tire options

Major Changes/Dates
New crankcase 8124-DHXA (replaced 8124-DHX) on engine IDCBM 5880, produced October 8, 1946

Comments
None

McCormick-Deering WDR-9

Engine D-335
Cylinders ....four
Bore and stroke ....4.4x5.5 inches
Displacement ....335 cubic inches
Rated rpm 1,500
Compression ratio 15.7:1
Ignition...IH H-4
Carburetor..IH model F-8
Cooling capacity ....11 gallons
Fuel tank capacity ....35 gallons, 7/8 gallon starting
Horsepower ratings
    Drawbar...48
    PTO/belt 53
Length...139 5/8 inches
Wheelbase..83 inches
Height ....82 3/4 inches (at top of muffler)
Width ....81 inches
Available treads ....62 inches (rear), 51 7/8 inches (front)
Weight ....7,230 pounds
Speed, forward, 15.00x34 tires

Gear	Speed
1	2 mph
2	3 3/8 mph
3	4 3/4 mph

```
4 ..................................................5 3/4 mph
5 ..................................................16 3/4 mph
Reverse ..........................................3 mph
```
Price $3,394 (1951)
Nebraska test number.....................................na
Numbers produced..na
Serial numbers ....see W-9 listing
Chassis prefixes WDR-9-RDCB
Engine prefixes..WDR-9-RDCBM
Chassis serial number location ....nameplate on right side of fuel tank support
Engine serial number location........................top milled section on left side of crankcase

Regular Equipment
Diesel engine, IH magneto, hand-operated over-center clutch, decelerator, front drawbar, steel wheels with spade lugs (6x4 inches), adjustable drawbar, and waterproof upholstered seat

Attachments and Special Features
Magneto ignition, hydraulic remote control, wheel scrapers for steel wheels, variable-tread rear rims for 15.00x34 tires, jute seat, radiator shutter, low-temp thermostat, hour meter, service meter, wheel weights, dual rear lamp, spark arrester, intake extension, exhaust extension, collector pre-cleaner, and pre-screener

Major Changes/Dates
First produced tractor (RDCB 14560) reported and probably produced August 18, 1945
New crankcase 8124-DHXA (replaced 8124-DHX) on tractor RDCBM 5896, produced October 16, 1946

Comments
None

McCormick-Deering WR-9
Engine C-335
Cylinders ....four
Bore and stroke ....4.4x5.5 inches
Displacement ....335 cubic inches
Rated rpm 1,500
Compression ratio...5.4:1
Ignition..IH H-4
Carburetor...1 3/8-inch IH E-13 updraft
Cooling capacity ....10 gallons
Fuel tank capacity ....36 gallons, 7/8 gallon starting
Horsepower ratings

Drawbar..47 gasoline, 44.5 distillate
PTO/belt ....52 gasoline, 49 distillate
Length..139 5/8 inches
Wheelbase...83 inches
Height ....83 7/8 inches
Width ....81 inches
Available treads ....62 inches (rear), 51 7/8 inches (front)
Weight ....6,895 pounds
Speed

Gear	Speed
1	2 mph
2	3 3/8 mph
3	4 3/4 mph
4	5 3/4 mph
5	16 3/4 mph
Reverse	3 mph

Price $2,953 (1951)
Nebraska test number....................................na
Numbers produced...na
Serial numbers ....see W-9 listing
Chassis prefixes ....RCB
Engine prefixes...RCBM
Chassis serial number location ....nameplate on fuel tank support
Engine serial number location.......................right side of engine crankcase

Regular Equipment

Distillate engine with radiator shutter, heat indicator, and manifold heat control, IH magneto, hand-operated over-center clutch, decelerator, front drawbar, steel wheels with spade lugs (6x4 inches), adjustable drawbar, and waterproof upholstered seat

Attachments and Special Features

Distillate engine, high-compression gasoline engine, high-altitude pistons, magneto ignition, hydraulic remote control, wheel scrapers for steel wheels, variable-tread rear rims for 15.00x34 tires, jute seat, radiator shutter, low-temp thermostat, hour meter, service meter, wheel weights, dual rear lamp, spark arrester, intake extension, exhaust extension, collector pre-cleaner, pre-screener, steel wheels, and a variety of wheel and tire equipment

Major Changes/Dates

Records are unclear, but first produced WR-9 tractor (RCB 14388) probably produced August 18, 1945

Comments

None

McCormick-Deering WR-9-S

Engine C-335
Cylinders ....four
Bore and stroke...4.4x5.5 inches
Displacement ....334.5 cubic inches
Rated rpm 1,500
Compression ratio 5.5:1
Ignition...6-volt distributor
Carburetor...1 1/4-inch IH Model E-12
Cooling capacity ....8 gallons
Fuel tank capacity ....36 gallons
Horsepower ratings
    Drawbar...38 steel, 47 rubber
    PTO/belt ....52 (IH)
Length...139 5/8 inches
Wheelbase...83 3/4 inches
Height..83 7/8 inches steel, 83 7/8 inches rubber
Width ....69 3/8 inches steel, 81 inches rubber
Available treads ....51 inches steel or 51 7/8 inches rubber (front); 57 3/8 inches steel or 62 inches rubber (rear)
Weight ....6,715 pounds steel, 6,720 pounds rubber
Speed
    Gear...*Speed (steel wheels; rubber tires)*
    1 ....2 5/8 mph; 2 mph
    2 ....3 mph; 3 3/8 mph
    3 ....4 7/8 mph; 4 3/4 mph
    4 ....4 7/8 mph; 4 3/4 mph
    5 ....na; 16 3/4 mph
    Reverse ....3 1/8 mph; 3 mph
Price ....na
Nebraska test number.....................................na
Numbers produced..na
Serial numbers
    1953 501–549
    1954 550–721
    1955 722–754
    1956 755–770
    1957 771–779
Chassis prefixes WR-9S
Engine prefixes..RCBM
Chassis serial number location ....on nameplate on right side of fuel tank support
Engine serial number location........................on pad on right side of engine above ignition unit

Regular Equipment

Information not available

Attachments and Special Features

Hydraulic remote control, belt pulley, air intake and exhaust extensions, collector pre-cleaner, swinging drawbar, muffler, PTO, combination rear work and travel lamp, foam rubber upholstered seat, spark arrester, wheel weights, engine hour meter, high-altitude pistons, rear wheel scrapers for steel wheels, magneto ignition, and distillate engine

Major Changes/Dates

Information not available

Comments

No attempt was made at the factory to match engine and chassis serial numbers

Updike lists 755–779 in 1956

McCormick-Deering Super WD-9 and Super WDR-9

Engine	D-350 vertical inline diesel
Cylinders	four
Bore and stroke	4.5x5.5 inches
Displacement	350 cubic inches
Rated rpm	1,500
Compression ratio	15.61:1
Ignition	12-volt battery and distributor (starting)
Carburetor	3/4-inch IH model F-8 (gas starting only)
Cooling capacity	9 gallons
Fuel tank capacity	35 gallons
Horsepower ratings	
Drawbar	58 (IH)
PTO/belt	64 (IH)
Length	83 inches
Wheelbase	83 3/8 inches

SUPER WD-9

The Super WD-9 was intended for the heaviest of tillage duties on large farms. The Super WD-9 featured IH's unique start-on-gas diesel engines. *State Historical Society of Wisconsin*

Height ....82 3/4 inches
Width ....81 inches
Available treads ....66 inches (rear), 52 inches (front)
Weight ....7,055 pounds
Speed

Gear	Speed
1	2 3/8 mph
2	3 1/8 mph
3	4 mph
4	5 mph
5	15 3/4 mph
Reverse	3 mph

Price ....na
Nebraska test number....................................518
Numbers produced

1953	4,773
1954	3,662
1955	1,830
1956	673

Serial numbers

1953	501–1934
1954	1935–5231
1955	5232–6863
1956	6864–7232 (SWD) or 6866–7242 (SWDR)

Chassis prefixes ....SWD-9 and SWDR-9
Engine prefixes...D-350
Chassis serial number location ....on nameplate on fuel tank support
Engine serial number location.......................top milled section on left side of engine crankcase

Regular Equipment
     Information not available

Attachments and Special Features
     Steel wheels available on WDR-9; Bosch or IH injection pump available

Major Changes/Dates
     Information not available

Comments
     No attempt was made by the factory to match engine and tractor serial numbers

Farmall 100

Engine..C-123
Cylinders ....four

Bore and stroke ....3 1/8x4 inches
Displacement ....123 cubic inches
Rated rpm 900–1,400
Compression ratio 6.48:1
Ignition...6-volt battery
Carburetor...Carter or Zenith 67x7
Cooling capacity ....3 3/4 gallons
Fuel tank capacity ....11 gallons
Horsepower ratings
    Drawbar..19
    PTO/belt 22
Length...107 inches
Wheelbase...71 inches
Height ....65 inches (at top of steering wheel)
Width ....56 inches (with rear wheels in), 78 inches (with rear wheels out)
Available treads ....40–68 inches (rear; 4-inch intervals), 44–64 inches (front)
Weight ....2,600 pounds without fuel or water
Speed

Gear	Speed
1	2.32 mph
2	3.68 mph
3	4.84 mph
4	10.05 mph
Reverse	2.9 mph

Price ....na
Nebraska test number....................................537
Numbers produced (includes 100 High Clearance, International 100)
    1954 and 1955 9,990
    1956 8,585
    17,383 Farmall 100s produced
Serial numbers
    1954 501–1719
    1955 1720–12894
    1956 12895–18940
Chassis prefixes 100
Engine prefixes..C-123
Chassis serial number location ....plate on left side of clutch housing
Engine serial number location......................right side of crankcase above ignition unit

Regular Equipment
    Fast Hitch, Touch Control, adjustable front axle, fenders, nonadjustable front wheels, battery ignition, starter and lights, muffler, spring-mounted non-upholstered seats, 9.00x24 rear tires, and 5.00x15 front tires

Attachments and Special Features

Adjustable wide-tread front axle, air pipe extension, Allied Equipment coupling beam, belt pulley and PTO, angle-belt pulley and take off, break-away electrical connector, combination rear lamp and taillight, exhaust valve rotators, distillate- and kerosene-burning equipment, hydraulic remote control, high-altitude pistons, pre-screener, radiator shutter, seed-plate drive, wheel weights, fast-hitch cushion spring, adjustable front wheels, deluxe foam rubber seat, detachable seat pad, auxiliary drawbar, pintle-hook drawbar, swinging drawbar, muffler, Hydra-Creeper, low-boiling-point thermostat and heat indicator, pneumatic tire pump, pre-cleaner, safety light, Touch Control, and Touch Control conversion package (for AI-23 Highway Mower)

Major Changes/Dates

Information not available

Comments

None

Farmall 100 High Clearance

Engine	C-123
Cylinders	four
Bore and stroke	3 1/8x4 inches
Displacement	123 cubic inches
Rated rpm	900–1,400
Compression ratio	6.48:1
Ignition	6-volt battery
Carburetor	Carter or Zenith 67x7
Cooling capacity	3 3/4 gallons
Fuel tank capacity	11 gallons
Horsepower ratings	
Drawbar	22
PTO/belt	19
Length	115 inches
Wheelbase	71 5/8 inches
Height	71 3/4 inches
Width	60 5/8 inches (with rear wheels in), 77 3/4 inches (with rear wheels out)
Available treads	48–68 inches (rear; 4-inch intervals), 43 3/4 to 67 3/4 inches basic (front)
Weight	2,825 pounds (no fuel or water)
Speed	

Gear	Speed
1	2.96 mph
2	4.7 mph
3	6.19 mph
4	12.85 mph

Reverse ....3.71 mph
Price ....na
Nebraska test number....................................na
Numbers produced...1,057
Serial numbers ....see Farmall 100 listing
Chassis prefixes 100-HC
Engine prefixes...C-123
Chassis serial number location ....plate on left side of clutch housing
Engine serial number location.......................right side of crankcase above ignition unit

Regular Equipment

Fast Hitch, Touch Control, adjustable front axle, fenders, nonadjustable front wheels, battery ignition, starter and lights, muffler, spring-mounted non-upholstered seats, 9.00x24 rear tires, and 5.00x15 front tires

Attachments and Special Features

Belt pulley and PTO, air pipe extension, combination rear lamp and taillight, exhaust valve rotators, distillate- and kerosene-burning equipment, hydraulic remote control, high-altitude pistons, pre-screener, radiator shutter, seed-plate drive, wheel weights, fast-hitch cushion spring, adjustable front wheels, and deluxe foam rubber seat

Major Changes/Dates

Information not available

Comments

None

International 100

Engine C-123
Cylinders ....four
Bore and stroke ....3 1/8x4 inches
Displacement ....123 cubic inches
Rated rpm 1,400
Compression ratio...na
Ignition...6-volt battery
Carburetor...Carter or Zenith 67x7
Cooling capacity ....15 quarts
Fuel tank capacity ....11 gallons
Horsepower ratings.......................................na
Length...106 7/8 inches
Wheelbase..71 1/8 inches
Height ....81 3/4 inches (at top of muffler), 64 1/4 inches (at steering wheel)
Width ....55 7/8 inches minimum, 78 inches maximum

Available treads ....44–64 inches (4-inch intervals)
Weight ....na
Speed, forward, 9.00x24 tires
    Gear..*Speed*
    1 ....2.3 mph
    2 ....3.7 mph
    3 ....4.8 mph
    4 ....10.0 mph
    Reverse ....2.9 mph
Price ....na
Nebraska test number...................................na
Numbers produced.......................................135
Serial numbers
    1954 501–503
    1955 504–574
    1956 575–635
Chassis prefixes 100
Engine prefixes...C-123
Chassis serial number location ....plate on left side of clutch housing
Engine serial number location......................right side of crankcase above igni-
                                                   tion unit

Regular Equipment
Information not available

Attachments and Special Features
Adjustable wide-tread front axle, air pipe extension, allied equipment coupling beam, belt pulley and PTO, angle-belt pulley and take off, breakaway electrical connector, combination rear lamp and taillight, exhaust valve rotators, distillate- and kerosene-burning equipment, hydraulic remote control, high-altitude pistons, pre-screener, radiator shutter, seed-plate drive, wheel weights, fast-hitch cushion spring, adjustable front wheels, deluxe foam rubber seat, detachable seat pad, auxiliary drawbar, pintle-hook drawbar, swinging drawbar, muffler, Hydra-Creeper, low-boiling-point thermostat and heat indicator, pneumatic tire pump, pre-cleaner, safety light, Touch Control, and Touch Control conversion package (for AI-23 Highway Mower)

Major Changes/Dates
Information not available

Comments
None

Farmall 130
Engine...C-123
Cylinders ....four
Bore and stroke...3 1/8x4 inches

Displacement ....122.7 cubic inches
Rated rpm 1,450
Compression ratio...6.8:1
Ignition...6-volt battery
Carburetor..7/8-inch Carter or Zenith 67x7
Cooling capacity ....15 quarts
Fuel tank capacity ....11 gallons
Horsepower ratings
   Drawbar...21.09 (Nebraska corrected maximum)
   PTO/belt ....23.11 (Nebraska corrected maximum)
Length...107 inches
Wheelbase...71 inches
Height ....65 inches (at steering wheel)
Width ....56 inches (with wheels in), 78 inches (with wheels out)
Available treads ....40–68 inches (rear; 4-inch intervals), 44–64 inches (front)
Weight ....2,650 pounds (no fluids)
Speed

Gear	Speed
1	2.32 mph
2	3.68 mph
3	4.84 mph
4	10.05 mph
Reverse	2.9 mph

Price ....na
Nebraska test number....................................617
Numbers produced (includes 130 High Clearance, International 130)
   1956 and 1957 6,946
   1958 2,821
   9,197 Farmall 130s produced
Serial numbers
   1956..501–1119
   1957..1120–8362
   1958..8363–10209
Chassis prefixes 130
Engine prefixes..C-123
Chassis serial number location ....left side of clutch housing
Engine serial number location.........................right side of engine above ignition unit

Regular Equipment

Fast Hitch, Touch Control, adjustable or nonadjustable front axle, fenders, nonadjustable front axles, battery ignition, starter and lights, muffler, spring-mounted non-upholstered seats, 9.00x24 rear tires, and 5.00x15 front tires

Attachments and Special Features

Belt pulley and PTO, engine PTO, air pipe extension, combination rear lamp and taillight, exhaust valve rotators, distillate- and kerosene-burning equipment, hydraulic remote control, high-altitude pistons, pre-screener, radiator shutter, wheel weights, fast-hitch cushion spring, adjustable front wheels, deluxe foam rubber seat, Hydra-Creeper, fuel-gauge filler cap, seed-plate drive, safety light, drawbar pintle-hook, and breakaway electric socket; also available without Touch Control, with magneto ignition, and with nonadjustable front axle

Major Changes/Dates
Information not available

Comments
None

Farmall 130 High Clearance

Engine	C-123
Cylinders	four
Bore and stroke	3 1/8x4 inches
Displacement	123 cubic inches
Rated rpm	1,400
Compression ratio	6.8:1
Ignition	6-volt battery
Carburetor	Carter or Zenith 67x7
Cooling capacity	15 quarts
Fuel tank capacity	11 gallons
Horsepower ratings	na
Length	115 inches
Wheelbase	71 5/8 inches
Height	71 3/4 inches (at steering wheel)
Width	60 5/8 inches (with wheels in), 77 3/4 inches (with wheels out)
Available treads	48–68 (rear; 4-inch intervals), 43 3/4 to 67 3/4 inches (front)
Weight	2,800 pounds (no fluids)

Speed

Gear	Speed
1	3.05 mph
2	4.84 mph
3	6.37 mph
4	13.2 mph
Reverse	3.81 mph

Price	na
Nebraska test number	na
Numbers produced	1,057
Serial numbers	see Farmall 130 listing
Chassis prefixes	130HC
Engine prefixes	C-123

Chassis serial number location ....left side of clutch housing
Engine serial number location.......................right side of crankcase above ignition unit

Regular Equipment

Fast Hitch, Touch Control, adjustable or nonadjustable front axle, fenders, battery ignition, starter and lights, muffler, spring-mounted non-upholstered seats, 9.00x36 rear tires, and 4.00x19 front tires

Attachments and Special Features

Belt pulley and PTO, engine PTO, air pipe extension, combination rear lamp and taillight, exhaust valve rotators, distillate- and kerosene-burning equipment, hydraulic remote control, high-altitude pistons, pre-screener, radiator shutter, wheel weights, fast-hitch cushion spring, adjustable front wheels, deluxe foam rubber seat, Hydra-Creeper, fuel-gauge filler cap, seed-plate drive, safety light, drawbar pintle-hook, and breakaway electric socket; also available without Touch Control, with magneto ignition, and with nonadjustable front axle

Major Changes/Dates

Information not available

Comments

Provides 27 inches of crop clearance versus 21 7/8 inches for regular Farmall 130

International 130

Engine..C-123 vertical inline
Cylinders ....four
Bore and stroke...3 1/8x4 inches
Displacement ....123 cubic inches
Rated rpm 1,400
Compression ratio...6.8:1
Ignition...6-volt battery
Carburetor..7/8-inch Carter or Zenith 67x7 updraft
Cooling capacity ....15 quarts
Fuel tank capacity ....11 gallons
Horsepower ratings
    Drawbar ....15.82 (Nebraska, 75 percent of max)
    PTO/belt..19.64 (Nebraska, 85 percent of max)
Length...107 inches
Wheelbase..71 inches
Height ....65 inches (at steering wheel)
Width ....78 inches (with wheels set out), 56 inches (with wheels set in)
Available treads..40–68 inches (rear), 44–70 inches (front)

173

Weight ....2,650 pounds (no fluids)
Speed
   Gear..*Speed*
   1 ....2.3 mph
   2 ....3.6 mph
   3 ....4.8 mph
   4 ....10 mph
   Reverse ....2.9 mph
Price ....na
Nebraska test number....................................na
Numbers produced..na
Serial numbers ....na
Chassis prefixes ....na
Engine prefixes..C-123
Chassis serial number location ....left side of clutch housing
Engine serial number location............................right side of engine above ignition unit

Regular Equipment

Touch control, adjustable front axle, fenders, nonadjustable front wheels, battery ignition, starter and lights, muffler, spring-mounted non-upholstered seat, 9.00x24 rear tires, and 5.00x15 front tires

Attachments and Special Features

Belt pulley and PTO, engine PTO, air pipe extension, combination rear lamp and taillight, exhaust valve rotators, distillate- and kerosene-burning equipment, hydraulic remote control, high-altitude pistons, pre-screener, radiator shutter, wheel weights, fast-hitch cushion spring, adjustable front wheels, deluxe foam rubber seat, Hydra-Creeper, fuel-gauge filler cap, seed-plate drive, safety light, drawbar pintle-hook, breakaway electric socket; also available without Touch Control, with magneto ignition, and with nonadjustable front axle

Major Changes/Dates

Information not available

Comments

None

Farmall 200

Engine ....C123 inline upright, overhead valves
Cylinders ....four
Bore and stroke ....3 1/8x4 inches
Displacement ....123 cubic inches
Rated rpm 1,650
Compression ratio...6.48:1
Ignition..6-volt battery

FARMALL 200
The Farmall 200, which replaced the Super C, was fitted with live hydraulics and Fast-Hitch. Notice that the wheels are set out on the axle and dished out as far as possible. On the Hundred Series tractors, the sheet metal was restyled and other minor changes made. *State Historical Society of Wisconsin*

Carburetor	Carter or Zenith 67x7
Cooling capacity	15 quarts
Fuel tank capacity	11 gallons, 7/8 gallon starting
Horsepower ratings	
Drawbar	22 (IH)
PTO/belt	25 (IH)
Length	123 inches
Wheelbase	82 1/4 inches
Height	74 3/4 inches (at steering wheel)
Width	90 3/4 inches (wheels), 80 inches (axles)
Available treads	48–80 inches (regular rear axles), 48–88 inches (88-inch-tread rear axle), or 56–100 inches (100-inch-tread rear axle)
Weight	3,160 pounds (no fluids)
Speed	
Gear	*Speed*
1	2 mph
2	3 7/8 mph
3	5 1/8 mph
4	10 5/8 mph
Reverse	3 1/8 mph
Price	na
Nebraska test number	536
Numbers produced	
1954 and 1955	7,576
1956	6,150
Serial numbers	
1954	501–1031
1955	1032–10903
1956	10904–15698
Chassis prefixes	na
Engine prefixes	C-123

Chassis serial number location ....left side of clutch housing
Engine serial number location......................right side of engine crankcase above crankcase breather

Regular Equipment

Gasoline engine, nonadjustable front wheels, double-disc foot-operated differential brakes, governor, heat indicator, battery ignition, starter, lights, muffler, 48-88 rear tread, hydraulic non-upholstered seat, 10.00x36 rear tires, 5.00x15 front tires, hydraulic Touch Control, and Fast Hitch

Attachments and Special Features

Adjustable-tread double front wheels, wheel weights, rear wheel fenders, pre-cleaner, air pipe extension, rear axles for 88- or 100-inch tread, single front wheel, upholstered seat with foam rubber cushion, combination rear and taillamp, pre-screener for air cleaner, pneumatic tire pump, distillate burning engine with radiator shutter, spark arrester, exhaust extension, exhaust valve rotators, PTO, combination PTO and belt pulley, swinging drawbar, hydraulic remote control, hour meter, 7-mph 3rd gear, tilt-back seat bracket, magneto ignition, and high-altitude pistons; also available without Fast Hitch, Touch Control, and Hydra-Creeper

Major Changes/Dates

Information not available

Comments

None

Farmall 230

Engine ....C-123 vertical inline
Cylinders ....four
Bore and stroke ....3 1/4x4 inches
Displacement ....123 cubic inches
Rated rpm 1,800
Compression ratio..6.8:1
Ignition..6-volt battery
Carburetor...7/8-inch
Cooling capacity ....15 quarts
Fuel tank capacity ....11 gallons, 7/8 gallon starting
Horsepower ratings
    Drawbar...19.4 (Nebraska, 75 percent of max)
    PTO/belt..24.84 (Nebraska, 85 percent of max)
Length..123 inches
Wheelbase...82 1/4 inches
Height ....74 3/4 inches steering
Width ....90 3/4 inches (with rear wheels out), 80 inches (axles)
Available treads ....48– 80 inches (rear), 6 5/8 to 12 5/8 inches (front)

Weight ....3,100 pounds
Speed
    Gear..*Speed*
    1 ....2.7 mph
    2 ....4.3 mph
    3 ....5.6 mph
    4 ....11.7 mph
    Reverse ....3.4 mph
Price ....na
Nebraska test number....................................616
Numbers produced
    1956 and 1957 5,489
    1958..1,973
Serial numbers
    1956..501–814
    1957..815–6826
    1958..6827–7671
Chassis prefixes ....na
Engine prefixes...C-123
Chassis serial number location ....plate on left side of clutch housing
Engine serial number location.......................right side of engine crankcase above ignition unit

Regular Equipment
Gasoline engine, nonadjustable front wheels, double-disc foot-operated differential brakes, heat indicator, battery ignition, starter, lights, muffler, 48-80 rear tread, hydraulic non-upholstered seat, 11.20x36 rear tires, 5.00x15 front tires, one-valve Hydra Touch, and Fast Hitch with Traction Control

Attachments and Special Features
Adjustable-tread double front wheels, adjustable wide front axles, two-valve Hydra Touch, wheel weights, rear wheel fenders, pre-cleaner, air pipe extension, rear axles for 88- or 100-inch maximum treads, single front wheel, upholstered seat with foam rubber cushion, combination rear lamp and tail-lamp, safety light, extension cord, breakaway electrical connector, pre-screener, distillate burning engine with radiator shutter, spark arrester, exhaust valve rotators, PTO, combination PTO and belt pulley, hydraulic remote control, hour meter, 7-mph 3rd gear, tilt-back seat bracket, fuel-gauge filler cap, swinging drawbar instead of Fast Hitch, drawbar extension plate, high-altitude pistons, and magneto ignition; available without Fast Hitch and Hydra-Creeper

Major Changes/Dates
Information not available

Comments
None

Farmall 300

Engine C-169
Cylinders ....four
Bore and stroke ....3 9/16x4 1/4 inches
Displacement ....169 cubic inches
Rated rpm 1,750
Compression ratio 6.6:1
Ignition...6-volt battery
Carburetor..1 1/4-inch IH updraft
Cooling capacity ....4 1/8 gallons
Fuel tank capacity ....17 gallons
Horsepower ratings
   Drawbar..33
   PTO/belt 37.5
Length..136 inches (tricycle), 140 inches
   (wide front)
Wheelbase..92 1/4 inches (tricycle), 96 inches
   (wide front)
Height..77 inches (at steering wheel)
Width ....100 inches (rear wheels), 83 inches
   (rear axles)
Available treads ....48–88 inches (rear), 48–100 inches
   (optional rear axle), 8 1/8 to 16 3/4
   inches (tricycle front), 57 to 89 3/4
   inches optional (wide front)
Weight ....4,700 pounds (no fluids)
Speed

Gear	Speed	
	regular	with TA
1	2.500 mph	1.685 mph
2	3.825 mph	2.585 mph
3	5.155 mph	3.485 mph
4	6.605 mph	4.455 mph
5	16.115 mph	10.875 mph
Reverse	3.125 mph	2.105 mph

Price ....na
Nebraska test number.....................................538
Numbers produced (includes 300 High Clearance)
   1954 and 1955 19,466
   1956...10,528
   29,501 Farmall 300s produced
Serial numbers
   1954 ....501–1778 or 501–3359
   1955 ....1779–23223 or 3360–23223
   1956 ....23224–29578 or 30508
Chassis prefixes ....F300, "L" added for LPG
Engine prefixes...C-169

Chassis serial number location ....plate on right side of clutch housing
Engine serial number location.....................right side of crankcase above
                                                  crankcase vent

Regular Equipment

Gasoline engine, TA, deluxe foam rubber seat with tilt-back bracket, vertically adjustable drawbar, electric starter and lights with combination rear lamp and taillight, two-valve Hydra Touch, muffler, variable-tread dual front wheels, 11.00x38 rear tires, and 5.50x16 front tires

Attachments and Special Features

Independent PTO, Fast Hitch, three-valve Hydra Touch, remote-control attachment, belt pulley, single front wheel, adjustable-tread wide front axle, 100-inch rear axles, right rear axle extension, wheel weights, fast-hitch swinging drawbar, swinging drawbars for tractors without Fast Hitch, left-side junction box for two-valve Hydra Touch, frame channel weights, spark arrester, air intake extension, exhaust pipe extension, low underslung exhaust, fenders, radiator shutter, high-altitude pistons, pre-screener, magneto ignition, cigarette lighter, distillate engine, non-upholstered non-tilt seat, nonadjustable front wheels, safety light, and break-away electrical connector; could be purchased without Hydra Touch

Major Changes/Dates

Information not available

Comments

None

Farmall 300 High Clearance

Engine	C-169
Cylinders	four
Bore and stroke	3 9/16x4 1/4 inches
Displacement	169 cubic inches
Rated rpm	1,750
Compression ratio	6.6:1
Ignition	6-volt battery
Carburetor	1 1/4-inch IH updraft
Cooling capacity	4 1/8 gallons
Fuel tank capacity	17 gallons
Horsepower ratings	
Drawbar	33 (IH)
PTO/belt	37.5
Length	152 3/8 inches
Wheelbase	97 3/8 inches
Height	88 inches (at steering wheel)
Width	85 7/8 inches
Available treads	69 inches (rear), 60 1/4 to 84 1/4 inches (front)

Weight ....6,025 (no fluids)
Speed
   Gear.........................Speed
   ....regular........................with TA
   1 ....2.4 mph......................1.62 mph
   2 ....3.67 mph....................2.48 mph
   3 ....4.96 mph....................3.34 mph
   4 ....6.35 mph....................4.28 mph
   5 ....15.49 mph................10.45 mph
   Reverse ....3.00 mph..................2.02 mph
Price ....na
Nebraska test number....................................na
Numbers produced.......................................170
Serial numbers ....see Farmall 300 list
Chassis prefixes ....F300HC, "L" added for LPG
Engine prefixes..C-169
Chassis serial number location ....plate on right side of clutch housing
Engine serial number location.......................right side of crankcase above
                                                 crankcase vent

Regular Equipment

Gasoline engine, TA, deluxe foam rubber seat with tilt-back bracket, vertically adjustable drawbar, electric starter and lights with combination rear lamp and taillight, two-valve Hydra Touch, muffler, variable-tread dual front wheels, 11.00x38 rear tires, and 5.50x16 front tires

Attachments and Special Features

Independent PTO, Fast Hitch, three-valve Hydra Touch, remote-control attachment, belt pulley, wheel weights, fast-hitch swinging drawbar, quick-attachable high-hitch heavy-duty drawbar, left-side junction box for two-valve Hydra Touch, frame channel weights, spark arrester, air intake extension, exhaust pipe extension, low underslung exhaust, fenders, radiator shutter, high-altitude pistons, pre-screener, magneto ignition, cigarette lighter, distillate engine, non-upholstered non-tilt seat, nonadjustable front wheels, one-valve Hydra Touch, safety light, and break-away electrical connector; could be purchased without Hydra Touch and auxiliary stay rods

Major Changes/Dates

Information not available

Comments

None

International 300 Utility

Engine C-169
Cylinders ....four
Bore and stroke...3 9/16x4 1/4 inches

INTERNATIONAL 300 UTILITY

The 300 Utility was IH's first entry into the dedicated "Utility" tractor market that could be used in the field as well as for farmyard chores. The idea was based on Ford's N Series tractors, but the 300 Utility had unique IH touches, such as Torque Amplifier availability. *State Historical Society of Wisconsin*

Displacement	169 cubic inches
Rated rpm	1,750; some 2,000
Compression ratio	6.6:1
Ignition	6-volt battery
Carburetor	1 1/4-inch IH updraft
Cooling capacity	4 gallons
Fuel tank capacity	11 1/4 gallons
Horsepower ratings	
Drawbar	39.48 (IH)
PTO/belt	42.84 (IH)
Length	118 inches
Wheelbase	75 inches
Height	58 inches (at steering wheel)
Width	65 1/4 inches (over axles), 89 inches (with wheels out)
Available treads	48–76 inches (front and rear)
Weight	3,400 pounds (with water and fuel)

Speed, forward, 10.00x28 tires

Gear	Speed regular	with TA
1	2.4 mph	1.6 mph
2	3.6 mph	2.4 mph
3	4.9 mph	3.3 mph

```
4 ..........................6.3 mph......................4.2 mph
5 ..........................15.4 mph..................10.4 mph
Reverse ..................3 mph.......................2 mph
```
Price ....na
Nebraska test number....................................539 and 574 (LPG)
Numbers produced
```
1955 ......................................................14,312
1956 ......................................................18,864
```
Serial numbers
```
1955 ......................................................501–20218
1956 ......................................................20219–33664
```
Chassis prefixes I300
Engine prefixes..C-169
Chassis serial number location ....right side of clutch housing
Engine serial number location........................right side of engine above crankcase
breather

Regular Equipment

Double-disc foot-operated differential brakes, cigarette lighter, vertically adjustable drawbar, fenders, 48–76-inch adjustable front axle, governor, heat indicator, one-valve Hydra Touch, battery ignition, starter, underslung muffler, 48–78-inch adjustable rear axle, and spring-mounted non-upholstered seat

Attachments and Special Features

Pan seat with foam rubber cushion, spring-cushion seat with padded back rest, padded arm rests, swinging drawbar for regular and Fast Hitch, two front lights and one rear lamp, combination rear lamp and taillight, wheel weights, TA, independent PTO for TA tractors or with independent PTO front drive, transmission PTO for non-TA tractors, tachometer with hour meter, one or two additional-valve Hydra Touch, power steering, power-adjusted (rear wheels), belt pulley, front-mounted pulley for engine-driven PTO, magneto ignition, high-altitude pistons, safety light, break-away connector, and 24-foot extension cord

Major Changes/Dates

Muffler, clutch pedal and linkage, and hydraulic valves

Comments

Differential could be "flopped" to convert forward speeds to reverse and reverse to forward

International 330

Engine...C-135
Cylinders ....four
Bore and stroke..3 1/4x4 1/16 inches
Displacement ....134.8 cubic inches

Rated rpm 2,000
Compression ratio 7.3:1
Ignition..6-volt battery
Carburetor..7/8-inch Zenith 68x7 or Marvel
Schebler Model TSX-748
Cooling capacity ....14 quarts
Fuel tank capacity ....11 1/4 gallons
Horsepower ratings
  Drawbar...32.41 (IH)
  PTO/belt..35.24 (IH)
Length...117 inches
Wheelbase...73.5 inches
Height ....58.4 inches (at steering wheel)
Width ....88 inches (with rear wheels out), 64
inches (over rear axles)
Available treads ....48–76 inches (rear), 52–78 inches
(power adjust wheels), 48–76
inches (front)
Weight ....4,365 pounds (operating, with
options and 175-pound operator)
Speed, forward..11.00x28 rear tires

Gear	Speed	
	regular	with TA
1	2.497 mph	1.685 mph
2	3.821 mph	2.578 mph
3	5.153 mph	3.477 mph
4	6.602 mph	4.454 mph
5	16.108 mph	10.869 mph
Reverse	3.116 mph	2.103 mph

Price ....na
Nebraska test number....................................634
Numbers produced
  1957 and 58...4,261
Serial numbers
  1957 501–1487
  1958 1488–4763
Chassis serial number location ....plate on right side of clutch housing
Engine serial number location.......................right side of engine above distribu-
tor assembly

Regular Equipment
Differential-double-disc foot brakes, cigarette lighter, vertically adjustable drawbar, fenders, 48–76-inch adjustable front axle, heat indicator, 6-volt battery ignition and starter, underslung muffler, 48–76-inch rear tread, Hydra Touch reservoir, spring-mounted non-upholstered seat, tachometer, equipment for transmission-driven PTO, 5.50x16 front tires, and 11.00x28 rear tires

Attachments and Special Features

Belt pulley (for tractors with PTO), swinging drawbar, Fast Hitch with Traction Control and Pilot Guide (tractors with one-valve Hydra Touch), front-mounted PTO pulley, fuel-gauge filler cap, front-mounted hydraulic pump, Hydra Touch (one-, two-, or three-valve versions), two front lights and combination rear lamp and taillight, magneto in lieu of battery ignition, vertical muffler, high-altitude pistons, power steering (for tractors with Hydra Touch), PTO, independent PTO (for TA tractors or with drive parts mounted), transmission-driven PTO for tractors with or without TA, power-adjusted rear wheels (for 12.00x28 tires), deluxe cushioned seat, foam rubber seat, low-type seat with upholstered pan, arm rest pads, TA, three-point hitch adapter for Fast Hitch, wheel weights, front bolster weights, foot accelerator, heavy-duty fixed-tread front axle, pre-cleaner, exhaust valve rotators, and pre-screener

Major Changes/Dates

Information not available

Comments

No attempt made at factory to match engine and chassis serial numbers

Farmall 350

Engine	C-175 vertical inline (gas and LPG)
Cylinders	four
Bore and stroke	3 5/8x4 1/4 inches (gas and LPG)
Displacement	175 cubic inches (gas and LPG)
Rated rpm	1,750 (all)
Compression ratio	7:1 (gas), 9:1 (LPG)
Ignition and starting	12-volt battery and distributor
Carburetor	1 1/4-inch (gas and LPG)
Cooling capacity	19 quarts
Fuel tank capacity	17 gallons
Horsepower ratings	na
Length	136 inches
Wheelbase	92 1/4 inches
Height	77 3/8 inches (at steering wheel)
Width	83 inches minimum, 105 inches maximum
Available treads	48 to 93 inches (rear), 8 1/8 to 16 3/4 inches (front)
Weight	na

Speed

Gear	Speed	
	regular	with TA
1	2.5 mph	1.7 mph
2	3.8 mph	2.6 mph

3	5.2 mph	3.5 mph
4	6.6 mph	4.5 mph
5	16.1 mph	10.9 mph
Reverse	3.1 mph	2.1 mph

Price ....na
Nebraska test number....................................611
Numbers produced (includes diesels and High Clearances)
    1956 and 1957 11,855
    1958..4,950
    12,291 Farmall 350s produced
Serial numbers
    1956..501–1029
    1957..1030–14673
    1958..14674–17215
Chassis prefixes F350
Engine prefixes..C-175
Chassis serial number location ....plate on right side of clutch housing
Engine serial number location.......................right side of engine above crankcase breather

Regular Equipment
Information not available

Attachments and Special Features
Air pipe extension, auxiliary drawbar braces, belt pulley, cigarette lighter, cultivator stay rod anchor bracket, drawbar extension plate, quick-attachable fixed drawbar, swinging drawbar, exhaust muffler, exhaust pipe extension, Fast Hitch with Traction Control, fenders, wide-tread adjustable front axle, fuel-gauge filler cap, Hydra Touch system, hydraulic power steering, high-altitude pistons, independent or trans-mission-driven PTO, pre-cleaners, pre-screeners, wide-tread rear axle, rear axle extension, safety light, deluxe upholstered seat, detachable seat pad, seat springs, spark arrester, tachometer, tilt-back seat bracket, pneumatic tire pump, 12-volt conversion package, steel wheels, variety of wheel and tire equipment, and wheel weights

Major Changes/Dates
Information not available

Comments
Updike has same beginning and end dates, but different year breakouts

Farmall 350 Diesel
Engine...Continental D-193 inline diesel
Cylinders ....four
Bore and stroke...3 3/4x4 3/8 inches
Displacement ....193 cubic inches

Rated rpm 1,750
Compression ratio 16.87:1
Ignition...12-volt battery
Carburetor......................................na
Cooling capacity ....17 1/4 quarts
Fuel tank capacity ....17 gallons
Horsepower ratings
    Drawbar....................................36.76 (Nebraska corrected maximum)
    PTO/belt ....40.23 (Nebraska corrected maximum)
Length..136 inches
Wheelbase.......................................92 1/4 inches
Height ....77 7/8 inches (at steering wheel)
Width ....83 inches minimum, 105 inches maximum
Available treads ....48-93 inches (rear), 8 1/8 to 16 3/4 inches (front)
Weight ....5,365 pounds
Speed

Gear	Speed	
	regular	with TA
1	2.5 mph	1.7 mph
2	3.8 mph	2.6 mph
3	5.2 mph	3.5 mph
4	6.6 mph	4.5 mph
5	16.1 mph	10.9 mph
Reverse	3.1 mph	2.1 mph

Price ....na
Nebraska test number.....................609
Numbers produced..........................4,191
Serial numbers ....see Farmall 350 listing
Chassis prefixes ....na
Engine prefixes................................D-193
Chassis serial number location ....plate on right side of clutch housing
Engine serial number location.........left side of crankcase behind injection pump

Regular Equipment
    Information not available

Attachments and Special Features
    Belt pulley, cigarette lighter, cultivator stay rod anchor bracket, drawbar extension plate, quick-attachable fixed drawbar, swinging drawbar, exhaust muffler, exhaust pipe extension, Fast Hitch with Traction Control, adjustable-tread wide front axle, fenders, fuel-gauge filler cap, Hydra Touch system, hydraulic power steering, intake manifold air heater, pneumatic tire power-adjusted rear wheel and rim, PTO, pre-cleaners, pre-screeners, wide-tread rear axle, rear

axle extension, safety light, deluxe upholstered seat, detachable seat pads, seat springs, spark arrester, tachometer, tilt-back seat bracket, pneumatic tire pump, wheel weights, variety of wheel and tire equipment, and steel wheels

Major Changes/Dates
Information not available

Comments
None

Farmall 350 High Clearance

Engine	C-175
Cylinders	four
Bore and stroke	3 5/8x4 1/4 inches
Displacement	175 cubic inches
Rated rpm	1,750
Compression ratio	na
Ignition	na
Carburetor	na
Cooling capacity	19 quarts
Fuel tank capacity	17 gallons
Horsepower ratings	na
Length	152 3/8 inches
Wheelbase	97 1/4 inches
Height	88 3/4 inches
Width	85 7/8 inches
Available treads	60–90 inches (front), 62–74 inches (rear)
Weight	na

Speed, forward, 11.00x38 tires

Gear	Speed	
	regular	with TA
1	2.4 mph	1.6 mph
2	3.7 mph	2.5 mph
3	5.0 mph	3.3 mph
4	6.3 mph	4.3 mph
5	15.5 mph	10.5 mph
Reverse	3.0 mph	2.0 mph

Price	na
Nebraska test number	na
Numbers produced	151
Serial numbers	see Farmall 350 listing
Chassis prefixes	F350 HC
Engine prefixes	C-175
Chassis serial number location	plate on right side of clutch housing
Engine serial number location	right side of engine above crankcase breather

187

Regular Equipment
Information not available

Attachments and Special Features
Air pipe extension, auxiliary stay rods, belt pulley, cigarette lighter, drawbar extension plate, quick-attachable fixed drawbar, swinging drawbar, exhaust muffler, exhaust pipe extension, Fast Hitch with traction control, fenders, fuel-gauge filler cap, Hydra Touch system, hydraulic power steering, high-altitude pistons, independent or transmission-driven PTO, pre-cleaners, pre-screeners, safety light, deluxe upholstered seat, detachable seat pad, seat springs, spark arrester, tachometer, tilt-back seat bracket, pneumatic tire pump, 12-volt conversion package, variety of wheel and tire equipment, and wheel weights

Major Changes/Dates
Information not available

Comments
None

Farmall 350 Diesel High Clearance

Engine	Continental D-193 diesel
Cylinders	four
Bore and stroke	3 3/4x4 3/8 inches
Displacement	193 cubic inches
Rated rpm	1,750
Compression ratio	16.87:1
Ignition	diesel
Carburetor	none
Cooling capacity	17 1/4 quarts
Fuel tank capacity	17 gallons
Horsepower ratings	na
Length	152 3/8 inches
Wheelbase	97 1/4 inches
Height	88 3/4 inches (at steering wheel)
Width	85 7/8 inches
Available treads	60–90 inches (front), 62–74 inches (rear)
Weight	na

Speed, forward, 11.00x38 tires

Gear	Speed	
	regular	with TA
1	2.4 mph	1.6 mph
2	3.7 mph	2.5 mph
3	5.0 mph	3.3 mph
4	6.3 mph	4.3 mph
5	15.5 mph	10.5 mph

Reverse......................3.0 mph......................2.0 mph
Price..na
Nebraska test number...................................na
Numbers produced..21
Serial numbers...see Farmall 350 listing
Chassis prefixes..F350 DHL
Engine prefixes...D-193
Chassis serial number location......................plate on right side of clutch housing
Engine serial number location........................left side of crankcase behind injection pump

Regular Equipment
Information not available

Attachments and Special Features
Auxiliary stay rods, belt pulley, cigarette lighter, drawbar extension plate, quick-attachable high-hitch heavy-duty drawbar, quick-attachable fixed drawbar, exhaust muffler, exhaust pipe extension, Fast Hitch with Traction Control, fenders, fuel-gauge filler cap, Hydra Touch system, hydraulic power steering, intake manifold air heater, pneumatic tire power-adjusted rear wheel and rim, PTO, pre-cleaners, pre-screeners, safety light, deluxe upholstered seat, detachable seat pads, seat springs, spark arrester, tachometer, tilt-back seat bracket, pneumatic tire pump, and wheel weights

Major Changes/Dates
Information not available

Comments
Increased crop clearance under front axle from 19 inches to 34 inches, and rear axle from 25 inches to 35 5/8 inches

International 350 Utility

Engine...C175 (gas and LPG)
Cylinders...four
Bore and stroke...3 5/8x4 1/4 inches
Displacement...175 cubic inches (gas and LPG)
Rated rpm...2,000
Compression ratio...7.01:1
Ignition...6-volt battery
Carburetor..1 1/4-inch
Cooling capacity..18 quarts
Fuel tank capacity..11 1/4 gallons
Horsepower ratings
    Drawbar...40.57 (Nebraska corrected maximum)
    PTO/belt..44.94 (Nebraska corrected maximum)

Length..119 inches
Wheelbase.......................................75 inches
Height ....59 inches (at steering wheel)
Width ....64 inches minimum, 90 inches
                                                 maximum
Available treads ....48–76 inches (rear), 48–76 inches
                                                 (front), 52 inches (heavy-duty fixed
                                                 front axle)
Weight ....4,595 pounds
Speed

Gear	Speed regular	with TA
1	2.6 mph	1.8 mph
2	4.0 mph	2.7 mph
3	5.4 mph	3.6 mph
4	6.9 mph	4.6 mph
5	16.7 mph	11.3 mph
Reverse	3.2 mph	2.2 mph

Price ....na
Nebraska test number....................615
Numbers produced (includes diesels)
    1956 and 1957 13,575
    1958 4,950
    12,998 International 350 Utilities produced
Serial numbers
    1956 ....501–1962 or 1977
    1957 ....1963–15048 or 1978–15050
    1958 ....15049–18346 or 15051–18346
Chassis prefixes I-350
Engine prefixes..............................C-175
Chassis serial number location ....plate on right side of clutch housing
Engine serial number location.......................right side of crankcase above
                                                 crankcase breather

Regular Equipment

Conventional vertically adjustable drawbar, one-valve Hydra Touch, transmission PTO drive, fenders, spring-mounted non-upholstered seat, 10.00x28 rear tires, 5.50x16 front tires, cigarette lighter, and tachometer

Attachments and Special Features

TA, Fast Hitch with Traction Control, 3x8 cylinder for Fast Hitch, two- and three-valve Hydra Touch, transmission-driven PTO, independent PTO, fan drive pulley for front-mounted PTO, lights, foam rubber upholstered pan-type seat, deep-cushion-type seat with padded backrest, arm rest pads for deep cushion seat, swinging drawbar for conventional drawbar, magneto, high-altitude pistons, wheel weights, power steering, fuel-gauge filler cap, power-adjusted wheels, orchard fenders, heavy-duty front axle, vertical muffler, and a variety of tires

Major Changes/Dates
Information not available

Comments
None

International 350 Diesel Utility

Engine	D-193 Continental diesel
Cylinders	four
Bore and stroke	3 3/4x4 3/8 inches
Displacement	193 cubic inches
Rated rpm	2,000
Compression ratio	16.87:1
Ignition	diesel, 12-volt starting system
Carburetor	none
Cooling capacity	4 gallons
Fuel tank capacity	11 1/4 gallons

Horsepower ratings

Drawbar	40.99 (Nebraska corrected maximum)
PTO/belt	44.10 (Nebraska corrected maximum)
Length	119 inches
Wheelbase	75 inches
Height	59 inches (at steering wheel)
Width	89 inches (rear wheels), 64 inches minimum
Available treads	48–76 inches (front and rear)
Weight	4,300 pounds (equipped, with operator)

Speed

Gear	Speed regular	with TA
1	2.6 mph	1.8 mph
2	4.0 mph	2.7 mph
3	5.4 mph	3.6 mph
4	6.9 mph	4.6 mph
5	16.7 mph	11.3 mph
Reverse	3.2 mph	2.2 mph

Price	na
Nebraska test number	610
Numbers produced	3,033
Serial numbers	see IH 350 listing
Chassis prefixes	I-350D
Engine prefixes	D-175

Chassis serial number location ....right side of clutch housing
Engine serial number location...........................right side of crankcase above breather

Regular Equipment

Conventional vertically adjustable drawbar, one-valve Hydra Touch, transmission PTO drive, fenders, spring-mounted non-upholstered seat, 10.00x28 rear tires, 5.50x16 front tires, cigarette lighter, and tachometer

Attachments and Special Features

TA, Fast Hitch with Traction Control, 3x8 cylinder for Fast Hitch, two- and three-valve Hydra Touch, transmission-driven PTO, independent PTO, fan drive pulley for front-mounted PTO, lights, foam rubber upholstered pan-type seat, deep-cushion-type seat with padded back rest, arm rest pads for deep cushion seat, swinging drawbar for conventional drawbar, wheel weights, power steering, fuel-gauge filler cap, power-adjusted wheels, orchard fenders, heavy-duty front axle, vertical muffler, variety of tires, and safety light

Major Changes/Dates
Information not available

Comments
None

International 350 Utility LPG

Engine C-175
Cylinders ....four
Bore and stroke ....3 5/8x4 1/4 inches
Displacement ....175 cubic inches
Rated rpm 2,000
Compression ratio..8.75:1
Ignition..12-volt battery
Carburetor...1 1/4-inch
Cooling capacity ....4 gallons
Fuel tank capacity ....18.4 gallons
Horsepower ratings
   Drawbar...42.87 (IH)
   PTO/belt..46.68 (IH)
Length...119 inches
Wheelbase...75 inches
Height ....59 inches
Width ....64 inches minimum, 89 inches maximum
Available treads ....48–76 inches (front and back)
Weight ....4,460 pounds equipped and with operator

Speed

Gear	Speed regular	with TA
1	2.6 mph	1.8 mph
2	4.0 mph	2.7 mph
3	5.4 mph	3.6 mph
4	6.9 mph	4.6 mph
5	16.7 mph	1.3 mph
Reverse	3.2 mph	2.2 mph

Price ....na
Nebraska test number....................................619
Numbers produced.......................................na
Serial numbers ....see IH 350 listing
Chassis prefixes ....na
Engine prefixes...C-175
Chassis serial number location ....right side of clutch housing
Engine serial number location.......................na

Regular Equipment

Conventional vertically adjustable drawbar, one-valve Hydra Touch, transmission PTO drive, fenders, spring-mounted non-upholstered seat, 10.00x28 rear tires, 5.50x16 front tires, cigarette lighter, and tachometer

Attachments and Special Features

TA, Fast Hitch with Traction Control, 3x8 cylinder for Fast Hitch, two- and three-valve Hydra Touch, transmission-driven PTO, independent PTO, fan drive pulley for front-mounted PTO, lights, foam rubber upholstered pan-type seat, deep-cushion-type seat with padded backrest, arm rest pads for deep cushion seat, swinging drawbar for conventional drawbar, magneto, high-altitude pistons, wheel weights, power steering, fuel-gauge filler cap, power-adjusted wheels, orchard fenders, heavy-duty front axle, vertical muffler, and a variety of tires

Major Changes/Dates

Information not available

Comments

None

International 350 Hi-Utility

Height ....64 inches (at steering wheel)
Speed, forward, 11.00x38 tires

Gear			Speed	
	regular 1750 rpm	with TA 1750 rpm	regular 2000 rpm	with TA 2000 rpm
1	2.8 mph	1.9 mph	2.5 mph	1.7 mph

2	4.3 mph	3.0 mph	3.8 mph	2.6 mph
3	5.9 mph	4.0 mph	5.2 mph	3.5 mph
4	7.9 mph	5.1 mph	6.6 mph	4.5 mph
5	18.4 mph	12.4 mph	16.1 mph	10.9 mph
Reverse	3.5 mph	2.4 mph	3.1 mph	2.1 mph

Comments

Hi-Utility had 25 inches of clearance, 5 inches more than regular 350s had. Dimensions, specifications, and options differ very little from other 350s—all engine options were available. The main differences were larger rear tires and longer front spindles.

International 350 Wheatland

Available treads ....53 inches (front)
Wheelbase...74 inches
Height ....60 inches (overall)
Speed, forward, 13.00x28 tires

Gear	regular	with TA	regular	with TA
	1750 rpm	1750 rpm	2000 rpm	2000 rpm
1	2.3 mph	1.6 mph	2.7 mph	1.8 mph
2	3.6 mph	2.4 mph	4.1 mph	2.8 mph
3	4.8 mph	3.3 mph	5.5 mph	3.7 mph
4	6.2 mph	4.2 mph	7.1 mph	4.8 mph
5	15.1 mph	10.2 mph	17.2 mph	11.6 mph
Reverse	2.9 mph	2.0 mph	3.3 mph	2.3 mph

Price ....na

Regular Equipment

Size 13.00x28 rear tires with W-12 rims and 6.00x16 front tires with 4.25 KA rims were recommended for use with these tractors

Attachments and Special Features

Independent PTO, fixed and swinging drawbars, and drawbar extension plate

Major Changes/Dates

Information not available

Comments

The IH 350 Wheatland was available with all the regular options of the normal IH 350s (including engine choices). The tractors had an increased ground clearance, heavy-duty, fixed-tread front axle; a high platform with large flat area; special fenders to provide increased protection from mud and dust; and a fixed, quick-adjustable drawbar.

Farmall 400

Engine	C-264
Cylinders	four
Bore and stroke	4x5 1/4 inches
Displacement	264 cubic inches
Rated rpm	900–1,450
Compression ratio	6.3:1
Ignition	na
Carburetor	1 1/4-inch IH
Cooling capacity	6 3/4 gallons
Fuel tank capacity	18 gallons

Horsepower ratings

Drawbar	45 (IH)
PTO/belt	51 (IH)
Length	141 1/8 inches (tricycle), 145 1/8 inches (wide front)
Wheelbase	95 3/4 inches (tricycle), 99 3/4 inches (wide axle)
Height	79 inches (at top of steering wheel)
Width	101 1/4 inches (rear wheels), 84 inches (rear axles)
Available treads	52–88 inches (rear), 52–100 inches (special rear axle), 8 3/8 to 17 inches (front)
Weight	5,950 pounds (no fluids)

Speed

Gear	Speed	(regular; with TA)
1	2.5 mph; 1.69 mph	
2	3.85 mph; 2.6 mph	
3	4.83 mph; 3.26 mph	
4	6.71 mph; 4.53 mph	
5	16.70 mph; 11.27 mph	
Reverse	3.33 mph; 2.35 mph	

Price	na
Nebraska test number	532 and 571 (LPG)

Numbers produced (includes diesels and High Clearances)

1954 and 1955	24,440
1956	16,517

31,806 Farmall 400s produced

Serial numbers

1954	501–4731 or 501–2587
1955	4732–29064 or 2588–29063
1956	29065–41484 or 29068–41485
Chassis prefixes	na
Engine prefixes	C-264
Chassis serial number location	left side of clutch housing
Engine serial number location	right side of engine above ignition unit

Regular Equipment

TA, deluxe foam rubber seat with tilt-back bracket, vertically adjustable drawbar, electric starter and lights with combination rear lamp and taillight, three-valve Hydra Touch, muffler, variable-tread dual front wheels, 12.00x38 rear tires, and 6.00x16 front tires

Attachments and Special Features

Available with one-, two-, or no-valve Hydra Touch, nonadjustable front wheels, non-upholstered non-tilt-back seat, independent PTO, Fast Hitch, hydraulic remote-control attachment, belt pulley, single front wheel, adjustable-tread wide front axle, 100-inch rear axle, wheel weights, fast-hitch swinging drawbar, swinging drawbar for tractors without Fast Hitch, left-side junction block for two-valve Hydra Touch, frame channel weights, spark arrester, air intake extension, exhaust pipe extension, low underslung exhaust, fenders, radiator shutter, high-altitude pistons, pre-screener, magneto ignition, cigarette lighter, variety of tires, tachometer, Electrall, and hydraulic power steering

Major Changes/Dates

Information not available

Comments

None

Farmall 400 High Clearance

Engine C-264
Cylinders ....four
Bore and stroke ....5x5 1/4 inches
Displacement ....264 cubic inches
Rated rpm 1,450
Compression ratio 6.3:1
Ignition..na
Carburetor..na
Cooling capacity ....6 3/4 gallons
Fuel tank capacity ....18 gallons
Horsepower ratings
   Drawbar..48.3 (IH)
   PTO/belt ....51 (IH)
Length..155 inches
Wheelbase...100 5/8 inches
Height ....93 inches at the steering wheel
Width ....85 7/8 inches
Available treads ....69 inches (rear), 60 1/4 to 84 1/4 inches (front)
Weight ....6,900 pounds no fuel or water

Speed

Gear	Speed	
	regular	with TA
1	2.64 mph	1.78 mph
2	4.07 mph	2.75 mph
3	5.10 mph	3.44 mph
4	7.10 mph	4.79 mph
5	17.66 mph	11.91 mph
Reverse	3.52 mph	2.38 mph

Price ....na
Nebraska test number....................................na
Numbers produced..143
Serial numbers ....see Farmall 400 listing
Chassis prefixes ....F-400 HC
Engine prefixes..C-264
Chassis serial number location ....left side of clutch housing
Engine serial number location.......................na

Regular Equipment

TA, deluxe foam rubber seat with tilt-back bracket, vertically adjustable drawbar, electric starter and lights with combination rear lamp and taillight, three-valve Hydra Touch, muffler, variable-tread dual front wheels, 13.00x38 rear tires, and 6.00x16 front tires

Attachments and Special Features

Available with one-, two-, or no-valve Hydra Touch, auxiliary stay rods, quick-attachable high-hitch heavy-duty drawbar, non-upholstered non-tilt-back seat, independent PTO, Fast Hitch, hydraulic remote-control attachment, belt pulley, wheel weights, fast-hitch swinging drawbar, swinging drawbar for tractors without Fast Hitch, left-side junction block for two-valve Hydra Touch, frame channel weights, spark arrester, air intake extension, exhaust pipe extension, low underslung exhaust, fenders, radiator shutter, high-altitude pistons, pre-screener, magneto ignition, cigarette lighter, variety of tires, and safety light

Major Changes/Dates

Information not available

Comments

None

Farmall 400 Diesel

Engine...D-264
Cylinders ....four
Bore and stroke...4x5 1/4 inches
Displacement ....264 cubic inches

Rated rpm 1,450
Compression ratio ....na
Ignition...na
Carburetor...na
Cooling capacity ....7 gallons
Fuel tank capacity ....18 gallons
Horsepower ratings
   Drawbar...43.9 (IH)
   PTO/belt ....48.3 (IH)
Length...141 1/8 inches (tricycle), 145 1/8
     inches (wide axle)
Wheelbase...95 3/4 inches (tricycle), 99 3/4
     inches (wide axle)
Height ....79 inches
Width ....101 1/4 inches (with rear wheels
     out), 84 inches (over rear axle)
Available treads ....52–88 inches (over rear axle),
     52–100 inches (wide rear axle), 8
     3/8 to 17 inches (front tricycle)
Weight ....6,785 pounds (no fuel or water)
Speed

Gear	Speed	
	regular	with TA
1	2.5 mph	1.69 mph
2	3.85 mph	2.6 mph
3	4.83 mph	3.26 mph
4	6.71 mph	4.53 mph
5	16.70 mph	11.27 mph
Reverse	3.33 mph	2.25 mph

Price $8,553
Nebraska test number.....................................534
Numbers produced..na
Serial numbers ....see Farmall 400 listing
Chassis prefixes ....F-400 DHC
Engine prefixes...D-264
Chassis serial number location ....left side of clutch housing
Engine serial number location........................na

Regular Equipment

TA, deluxe foam rubber seat with tilt-back bracket, vertically adjustable drawbar, electric starter and lights with combination rear lamp and taillight, three-valve Hydra Touch, muffler, variable-tread dual front wheels, 12.00x38 rear tires, and 6.00x16 front tires

Attachments and Special Features

Available with one-, two-, or no-valve Hydra Touch, nonadjustable front wheels, non-upholstered, non-tilt-back seat, independent PTO, Fast

Hitch, hydraulic remote-control attachment, belt pulley, single front wheel, adjustable-tread wide front axle, 100-inch rear axle, wheel weights, fast-hitch swinging drawbar, swinging drawbar for tractors without Fast Hitch, left-side junction block for two-valve Hydra Touch, frame channel weights, spark arrester, air intake extension, exhaust pipe extension, low underslung exhaust, fenders, radiator shutter, pre-screener, magneto ignition, cigarette lighter, and a variety of tires.

Major Changes/Dates
Information not available

Comments
None

Farmall 400 Diesel High Clearance

Engine	D-264
Cylinders	four
Bore and stroke	4x5 1/4 inches
Displacement	264 cubic inches
Rated rpm	1,450
Compression ratio	
Ignition	na
Carburetor	na
Cooling capacity	7 gallons
Fuel tank capacity	18 gallons

Horsepower ratings

Drawbar	43.9
PTO/belt	48.5
Length	155 inches
Wheelbase	100 5/8 inches
Height	93 inches (at steering wheel)
Width	85 7/8 inches
Available treads	69 inches (rear), 60 1/4 to 84 1/4 inches (front)
Weight	7,235 pounds

Speed

Gear	Speed regular	with TA
1	2.64 mph	1.78 mph
2	4.07 mph	2.75 mph
3	5.10 mph	3.44 mph
4	7.10 mph	4.79 mph
5	17.66 mph	11.91 mph
Reverse	3.52 mph	2.38 mph

Price	na
Nebraska test number	na
Numbers produced	50
Serial numbers	see Farmall 400 listing

Chassis prefixes ....F-400 DHC
Engine prefixes...D-264
Chassis serial number location ....left side of clutch housing
Engine serial number location........................na

Regular Equipment

TA, deluxe foam rubber seat with tilt-back bracket, vertically adjustable drawbar, electric starter and lights with combination rear lamp and taillight, three-valve Hydra Touch, muffler, variable-tread dual front wheels, 13.00x38 rear tires, and 6.00x16 front tires

Attachments and Special Features

Available with one-, two-, or no-valve Hydra Touch, nonadjustable front wheels, non-upholstered, non-tilt-back seat, independent PTO, Fast Hitch, hydraulic remote-control attachment, belt pulley, single front wheel, adjustable-tread wide front axle, 100-inch rear axle, wheel weights, fast-hitch swinging drawbar, swinging drawbar for tractors without Fast Hitch, left-side junction block for two-valve Hydra Touch, frame channel weights, spark arrester, air intake extension, exhaust pipe extension, low underslung exhaust, fenders, radiator shutter, pre-screener, magneto ignition, cigarette lighter, and a variety of tires.

Major Changes/Dates

Information not available

Comments

None

Farmall 450

Engine..C-281
Cylinders ....four
Bore and stroke...4 1/8x5 1/4 inches
Displacement ....281 cubic inches
Rated rpm 1,450
Compression ratio...6.6:1
Ignition..6-volt battery
Carburetor...1 1/4-inch
Cooling capacity ....7 gallons
Fuel tank capacity ....21 gallons
Horsepower ratings
    Drawbar...51.25 (Nebraska max)
    PTO/belt..55.28 (Nebraska max)
Length..143 inches (tricycle), 147 inches (wide axle)
Wheelbase...95 3/4 inches (tricycle), 99 3/4 inches (wide front)
Height ....80 inches (at steering wheel)

FARMALL 450 AND 230

The Fifty and Thirty Series tractors were again restyled Hundred Series tractors, with minor changes. They are recognizable by their white painted grilles and the white decal on their sides, both of which set off the trade name letters. A 450 is in the foreground running the chopper, while a 230 is pulling the forage box. State Historical Society of Wisconsin

Width ....107 inches (rear wheels set out), 84 inches (rear axles)

Available treads ....50–94 inches (rear), 50–106 inches (wide rear axle), 8 3/8 to 17 inches (front)

Weight ....5,600 pounds (no fuel or water)

Speed

Gear	Speed regular	with TA
1	2.5 mph	1.7 mph
2	3.8 mph	2.6 mph
3	4.8 mph	3.2 mph
4	6.7 mph	4.5 mph
5	16.6 mph	11.2 mph
Reverse	3.3 mph	2.2 mph

Price ....na

Nebraska test number....................................612

Numbers produced (includes diesels and High Clearances)

    1956 and 1957 17,852

    1958 7,737

    18,305 Farmall 450s produced

Serial numbers

```
1956 .........................................................501–1733 or 2606
1957 .........................................................1734–18338 or 2607–22304
1958 .........................................................22305–26067
```
Chassis prefixes 450
Engine prefixes...C-281
Chassis serial number location ....left side of clutch housing
Engine serial number location.......................na

Regular Equipment

TA, deluxe foam rubber seat and tilt-back bracket, vertically adjusted drawbar, electric starter and lights with combination rear lamp and taillight, three-valve Hydra Touch, muffler, variable-tread dual front wheels, 13.60x38 rear tires, and 6.00x16 front tires

Attachments and Special Features

Independent PTO, Fast Hitch with Traction Control, belt pulley, single front wheel, adjustable-tread wide front axle, 106-inch rear axle, wheel weights, swinging drawbar for tractors without Fast Hitch, left-side junction block for two-valve Hydra Touch, frame channel weights, spark arrester, air intake extension, fenders, radiator shutter, high-altitude pistons, power-adjusted wheels, pre-screener, magneto ignition, cigarette lighter, fuel-gauge filler cap, power steering, three-point hitch to fast-hitch adapter, non-upholstered non-tilt seat back, one- or two-valve Hydra Touch (three standard), and nonadjustable front wheels; also available without Hydra Touch

Major Changes/Dates

Information not available

Comments

None

Farmall 450 Diesel

Engine D-281
Cylinders ....four
Bore and stroke..4 1/8x5 1/4 inches
Displacement ....281 cubic inches
Rated rpm 1,450
Compression ratio..17.45:1
Ignition..12-volt battery
Carburetor..3/4-inch
Cooling capacity ....30 quarts
Fuel tank capacity ....18 gallons
Horsepower ratings
    Drawbar..46.18 (Nebraska maximum)
    PTO/belt ....50.77 (Nebraska maximum)
Length...141 1/8 inches

Wheelbase	95 3/4 inches
Height	80 3/4 inches (at steering wheel)
Width	84 inches (over rear axles), 107 1/4 inches (with rear wheels out)
Available treads	50–94 inches (rear), 8 3/8 to 17 inches (front)
Weight	6,877 pounds

Speed

Gear	Speed	
	regular;	with TA
1	2.5 mph	1.7 mph
2	3.8 mph	2.6 mph
3	4.8 mph	3.2 mph
4	6.7 mph	4.5 mph
5	16.6 mph	11.2 mph
Reverse	3.3 mph	2 mph

Price	na
Nebraska test number	608
Numbers produced	6,961
Serial numbers	see Farmall 450 listing
Chassis prefixes	F-450 D
Engine prefixes	D-281
Chassis serial number location	left side of clutch housing
Engine serial number location	left side of engine above injection pump

Regular Equipment

TA, deluxe foam rubber seat and tilt-back bracket, vertically adjusted drawbar, electric starter and lights with combination rear lamp and taillight, three-valve Hydra Touch, muffler, variable-tread dual front wheels, 13.60x38 rear tires, and 6.0x16 front tires

Attachments and Special Features

Independent PTO, Fast Hitch with Traction Control, belt pulley, single front wheel, adjustable-tread wide front axle, 106-inch rear axle, wheel weights, swinging drawbar for tractors without Fast Hitch, left-side junction block for two-valve Hydra Touch, frame channel weights, spark arrester, air intake extension, fenders, radiator shutter, power-adjusted wheels, pre-screener, magneto ignition, cigarette lighter, fuel-gauge filler cap, power steering, three-point hitch to fast-hitch adapter, non-upholstered non-tilt seat back, one- or two-valve Hydra Touch (three standard), and nonadjustable front wheels; also available without Hydra Touch

Major Changes/Dates

Information not available

Comments
    None

Farmall 450 LPG

Engine..C-281
Cylinders ....four
Bore and stroke ....4 1/8x5 1/4 inches
Displacement ....281 cubic inches
Rated rpm 1,450
Compression ratio.......................................8.35:1
Ignition...12-volt battery
Carburetor..1 1/4-inch
Cooling capacity ....7 gallons
Fuel tank capacity ....28 gallons (at 80 percent full)
Horsepower ratings
    Drawbar..51.81 (Nebraska maximum)
    PTO/belt ....56.71 (Nebraska maximum)
Length...143 inches (tricycle), 147 inches
                                                                            (wide axle)
Wheelbase..95 3/4 inches (tricycle), 99 3/4
                                                                            inches (wide axle)
Height ....80 inches (at steering wheel)
Width ....107 inches (with rear wheels out),
                                                                            84 inches (over rear axle)
Available treads ....50–94 inches regular (rear), 50–106
                                                                            inches (special axle), 50–100 inches
                                                                            (power-adjusted rears), 50–112
                                                                            inches (special axle power adjust
                                                                            rears), 8 3/8 to 17 inches (front tricy-
                                                                            cle), 57–90 inches (wide front)
Weight ....6,000 pounds
Speed, forward, 13.60x38 tires
Gear ....Speed

	regular	with TA
1	2.5 mph	1.7 mph
2	3.8 mph	2.6 mph
3	4.8 mph	3.2 mph
4	6.7 mph	4.5 mph
5	16.6 mph	11.2 mph
Reverse	3.3 mph	2.2 mph

Price ....na
Nebraska test number.................................620
Numbers produced.......................................na
Serial numbers ....see Farmall 450 listing
Chassis prefixes ....na
Engine prefixes...C-281
Chassis serial number location ....left side of clutch housing

Engine serial number location......................na

Regular Equipment
TA, deluxe foam rubber seat and tilt-back bracket, vertically adjusted drawbar, electric starter and lights with combination rear lamp and taillight, three-valve Hydra Touch, muffler, variable-tread dual front wheels, 13.60x38 rear tires, and 6.00x16 front tires

Attachments and Special Features
Independent PTO, Fast Hitch with Traction Control, belt pulley, single front wheel, adjustable-tread wide front axle, 106-inch rear axle, wheel weights, swinging drawbar for tractors without Fast Hitch, left-side junction block for two-valve Hydra Touch, frame channel weights, spark arrester, air intake extension, fenders, radiator shutter, high-altitude pistons, power-adjusted wheels, pre-screener, magneto ignition, cigarette lighter, fuel-gauge filler cap, power steering, three-point hitch to fast-hitch adapter, non-upholstered non-tilt seat back, one- or two-valve Hydra Touch (three standard), and nonadjustable front wheels; also available without Hydra Touch

Major Changes/Dates
Information not available

Comments
None

Farmall 450 High Clearance

Engine...C-281
Cylinders ....four
Bore and stroke...4 1/2x5 1/4 inches
Displacement ....281 cubic inches
Rated rpm 1,450
Compression ratio.......................................6.6:1
Ignition...12-volt battery
Carburetor...1 1/4-inch IH updraft
Cooling capacity ....7 gallons (gas)
Fuel tank capacity ....21 gallons (gas)
Horsepower ratings
   Drawbar..51.25 (gas), 51.81 (LPG)
   PTO/belt ....57.05 (gas), 56.71 (LPG)
Length...155 inches
Wheelbase...100 3/8 inches
Height ....93 inches (at steering wheel)
Width...88 inches rear tires, 86 inches rear axles
Available treads ....62–74 inches (rear), 60–84 inches (front)
Weight ....6,600 (gas), 7,000 (diesel)

Speed

Gear	Speed	
	regular	with TA
1	2.6 mph	1.8 mph
2	4.1 mph	2.7 mph
3	5.1 mph	3.4 mph
4	7.1 mph	4.8 mph
5	17.7 mph	11.9 mph
Reverse	3.5 mph	2.4 mph

Price ....na
Nebraska test number......................................na
Numbers produced...55
Serial numbers ....see Farmall 450 listing
Chassis prefixes ....F-450 HC
Engine prefixes...C-281
Chassis serial number location ....left side of clutch housing
Engine serial number location.......................na

Regular Equipment

TA, deluxe foam rubber seat and tilt-back bracket, vertically adjusted drawbar, electric starter and lights with combination rear lamp and taillight, three-valve Hydra Touch, muffler, variable-tread dual front wheels, 13.00x38 rear tires, and 6.00x20 front tires

Attachments and Special Features

Independent PTO, Fast Hitch with Traction Control, belt pulley, single front wheel, adjustable-tread wide front axle, 106-inch rear axle, wheel weights, swinging drawbar for tractors without Fast Hitch, left-side junction block for two-valve Hydra Touch, frame channel weights, spark arrester, air intake extension, fenders, radiator shutter, high-altitude pistons, power-adjusted wheels, pre-screener, magneto ignition, cigarette lighter, fuel-gauge filler cap, power steering, three-point hitch to fast-hitch adapter, non-upholstered non-tilt seat back, one- or two-valve Hydra Touch (three standard), and nonadjustable front wheels; also available without Hydra Touch

Major Changes/Dates

Information not available

Comments

None

Farmall 450 Diesel High Clearance

Engine..D-281
Cylinders ....four
Bore and stroke..4 1/8x5 1/4 inches
Displacement ....281 cubic inches
Rated rpm 1,450

Compression ratio..17.45:1
Ignition..12-volt battery
Carburetor...3/4-inch
Cooling capacity ....30 quarts
Fuel tank capacity ....18 gallons
Horsepower ratings
    Drawbar..46.18 (Nebraska corrected maximum)
    PTO/belt ....50.77 (Nebraska corrected maximum)
Length..155 inches
Wheelbase...100 5/8 inches
Height ....93 inches (at steering wheel)
Width ....85 7/8 inches (at rear axle), 88 1/8
    inches (at rear wheels)
Available treads ....60 1/4 to 84 1/4 inches (front),
    62–74 inches (rear)
Weight ....7,000 pounds
Speed, forward, 13-38 tires

Gear	Speed	
	regular	with TA
1	2.6 mph	1.8 mph
2	4.1 mph	2.7 mph
3	5.1 mph	3.4 mph
4	7.1 mph	4.8 mph
5	17.7 mph	11.9 mph
Reverse	3.5 mph	2.4 mph

Price ....na
Nebraska test number.....................................na
Numbers produced..30
Serial numbers ....see Farmall 450 listing
Chassis prefixes ....F-450 DHC
Engine prefixes...D-281
Chassis serial number location ....left side of clutch housing
Engine serial number location........................na

Regular Equipment

    TA, deluxe foam rubber seat and tilt-back bracket, vertically adjusted drawbar, electric starter and lights with combination rear lamp and taillight, three-valve Hydra Touch, muffler, variable-tread dual front wheels, 13.00x38 rear tires, and 6.00x20 front tires

Attachments and Special Features

    Auxiliary stay rods, quick-attachable high-hitch heavy-duty drawbar, independent PTO, Fast Hitch with Traction Control, belt pulley, wheel weights, swinging drawbar for tractors without Fast Hitch, left-side junction block for two-valve Hydra Touch, frame channel weights, spark arrester, air intake extension, fenders, radiator shutter, power-adjusted wheels, pre-screener, magneto ignition, cigarette lighter, fuel-gauge filler cap, power steering, three-point hitch to fast-hitch adapter, non-uphol-stered non-tilt seat back, one- or two-valve Hydra Touch (three standard), and nonadjustable front wheels; also available without Hydra Touch

Major Changes/Dates
Information not available

Comments
None

International W-400

Engine	C-264
Cylinders	four
Bore and stroke	4x5 1/4 inches
Displacement	264 cubic inches
Rated rpm	1,450
Compression ratio	6.3:1
Ignition	12-volt battery
Carburetor	1 1/4 IH updraft
Cooling capacity	6 3/4 gallons
Fuel tank capacity	18 gallons

Horsepower ratings
Drawbar	47.38 (IH)
PTO/belt	53.24 (IH)
Length	130 inches
Wheelbase	82 inches
Height	93 3/8 inches
Width	75 3/4 inches
Available treads	50 3/4 inches (front), 60 1/4 inches (rear)
Weight	5,720 pounds (no fluids)

Speed

Gear	Speed	
	regular	with TA
1	2.4 mph	1.6 mph
2	3.7 mph	2.5 mph
3	4.7 mph	3.1 mph
4	6.5 mph	4.4 mph
5	16.1 mph	10.9 mph
Reverse	3.2 mph	2.2 mph

Price	na
Nebraska test number	433

Numbers produced (includes diesels)
1954 and 1955	1,336
1956	1,932

2,070 International W-400s produced

Serial numbers
    1954 501–509
    1955 ....510–2186 or 510–2191
    1956 2187–3858
Chassis prefixes W-400
Engine prefixes..C-264
Chassis serial number location ....left side of clutch housing
Engine serial number location.......................na

Regular Equipment

Battery ignition, starter, lights including combination rear light and taillamp, vertically adjustable drawbar, non-upholstered hydraulic seat, muffler, 14.00x30 rear tires, and 6.50x18 front tires

Attachments and Special Features

TA, power steering, independent or transmission PTO, swinging drawbar, deluxe foam rubber seat, Hydra Touch hydraulics, remote-control hydraulics (one, two, or three valves), air pipe extension, pre-screener, spark arrester, radiator shutter, wheel weights, service meter, and Electrall

Major Changes/Dates

Information not available

Comments

None

International W-400 Diesel

Engine D-264
Cylinders ....four
Bore and stroke ....4x5 1/4 inches
Displacement ....264 cubic inches
Rated rpm 900–1,450
Compression ratio..16.5:1
Ignition...12-volt battery
Carburetor..IH diesel-starting
Cooling capacity ....7 1/4 gallons
Fuel tank capacity ....18 gallons
Horsepower ratings
    Drawbar..42.24
    PTO/belt 48.56
Length..130 inches
Wheelbase..82 inches
Height ....91 3/4 inches (at top of muffler)
Width ....75 3/4 inches
Available treads..50 3/4 inches (front), 60 1/4 inches (rear)
Weight ....6,000 pounds (no fuel or water)

Speed

Gear ....Speed

..............................regular.......................with TA

1.................................2.4 mph.....................1.6 mph
2.................................3.7 mph.....................2.5 mph
3.................................4.7 mph.....................3.1 mph
4.................................6.5 mph.....................4.4 mph
5.................................16.1 mph...................10.9 mph
Reverse.......................3.2 mph.....................2.2 mph
Price ....na
Nebraska test number...................................535
Numbers produced..1,118
Serial numbers ....see IH W-400 listing
Chassis prefixes W-400-D
Engine prefixes...D-264
Chassis serial number location ....left side of clutch housing
Engine serial number location........................na

Regular Equipment

Battery ignition, starter, lights including combination rear light and taillamp, vertically adjustable drawbar, non-upholstered hydraulic seat, muffler, 14.00x30 rear tires, and 6.50x18 front tires

Attachments and Special Features

TA, power steering, independent or transmission PTO, swinging drawbar, deluxe foam rubber seat, Hydra Touch hydraulics, hydraulic remote control (one, two, or three valves), air pipe extension, pre-screener, spark arrester, radiator shutter, wheel weights, service meter, and Electrall

Major Changes/Dates

Information not available

Comments

None

International W-400 LPG

Engine..C-264
Cylinders ....four
Bore and stroke...4x5 1/4 inches
Displacement ....264 cubic inches
Rated rpm 900–1,450
Compression ratio..8.33:1
Ignition...6-volt battery
Carburetor...Ensign
Cooling capacity ....6 3/4 gallons
Fuel tank capacity ....31 gallons
Horsepower ratings

```
    Drawbar.....................................................48.85
    PTO/belt....................................................52.85
Length.............................................................130 inches
Wheelbase......................................................82 inches
Height ............................................................na
Width .............................................................75 3/4 inches
Available treads .............................................50 3/4 inches (front), 60 1/4 inches
                                                                (rear)
Weight ...........................................................6,000 pounds (no fuel or water)
Speed
```

Gear	Speed	
	regular	with TA
1	2.4 mph	1.6 mph
2	3.7 mph	2.5 mph
3	4.7 mph	3.1 mph
4	6.5 mph	4.4 mph
5	16.1 mph	10.9 mph
Reverse	3.2 mph	2.2 mph

```
Price ...............................................................na
Nebraska test number....................................572
Numbers produced.........................................na
Serial numbers ..............................................see IH W-400 listing
Chassis prefixes .............................................na
Engine prefixes...............................................C-264
Chassis serial number location ......................left side of clutch housing
Engine serial number location.......................na
```

Regular Equipment

Battery ignition, starter, lights including combination rear light and taillamp, vertically adjustable drawbar, non-upholstered hydraulic seat, muffler, 14.00x30 rear tires, and 6.50x18 front tires

Attachments and Special Features

TA, power steering, independent or transmission PTO, swinging drawbar, deluxe foam rubber seat, Hydra Touch hydraulics, hydraulic remote control (one, two, or three valves), air pipe extension, pre-screener, spark arrester, radiator shutter, wheel weights, service meter, and Electrall

Major Changes/Dates

Information not available

Comments

None

International W-450

```
Engine...........................................................C-281
Cylinders .......................................................four
```

Bore and stroke..4x5 1/4 inches
Displacement ....281 cubic inches
Rated rpm 1,450
Compression ratio...6.3:1
Ignition...12-volt battery
Carburetor...na
Cooling capacity ....6 3/4 gallons
Fuel tank capacity ....21 gallons
Horsepower ratings...na
Length...130 inches
Wheelbase...82 inches
Height ....93 3/8 inches
Width ....75 3/4 inches
Available treads ....50 3/4 inches (front), 60 1/4 inches (rear)
Weight ....5,720 pounds (no fuel or water)
Speed

Gear	Speed	
	regular	with TA
1	2.4 mph	1.6 mph
2	3.7 mph	2.5 mph
3	4.7 mph	3.1 mph
4	6.5 mph	4.4 mph
5	16.1 mph	10.9 mph
Reverse	3.2 mph	2.2 mph

Price ....na
Nebraska test number....................................na
Numbers produced (includes diesels)
   1956 and 1957 1,091
   1958...718
Serial numbers
   1956 501–567
   1957 568–1661
   1958...1662–2295
Chassis prefixes C-450
Engine prefixes...C-281 and D-281
Chassis serial number location ....plate on left side of clutch housing
Engine serial number location.......................right side of engine above crankcase breather

Regular Equipment

Battery ignition, starter, lights, including combination rear light and taillamp, vertically adjusted drawbar, non-upholstered hydraulic seat, muffler, 14.00x30 inch rear tires, and 6.50x18 front tires

Attachments and Special Features

TA, power steering, independent or transmission-type PTO, swinging drawbar, deluxe foam rubber seat, Hydra Touch, remote control (one, two, or three valves), air pipe extension, belt pulley, collector pre-cleaner, spark arrester, radiator shutter, wheel weights, service meter, Electrall, fuel-gauge filler cap, variety of tire equipment, variety of steel wheels, seat springs, safety light, and tachometer

Major Changes/Dates
Information not available

Comments
None

International W-450 LPG

Engine	C-281
Cylinders	four
Bore and stroke	4x5 1/4 inches
Displacement	281 cubic inches
Rated rpm	1,450
Compression ratio	8.35:1
Ignition	12-volt battery
Carburetor	1 1/4 Ensign
Cooling capacity	6 3/4 gallons
Fuel tank capacity	31 gallons
Horsepower ratings	na
Length	130 inches
Wheelbase	82 inches
Height	na
Width	75 3/4 inches
Available treads	50 3/4 inches (front), 60 1/4 inches (rear)
Weight	6,000 pounds (no fuel or water)

Speed

Gear	Speed	
	regular	with TA
1	2.4 mph	1.6 mph
2	3.7 mph	2.5 mph
3	4.7 mph	3.1 mph
4	6.5 mph	4.4 mph
5	16.1 mph	10.9 mph
Reverse	3.2 mph	2.2 mph

Price	na
Nebraska test number	na
Numbers produced	na
Serial numbers	see IH W-450 listing
Chassis prefixes	450
Engine prefixes	C-281
Chassis serial number location	left side of clutch housing

Engine serial number location.......................left side of engine above injection pump

Regular Equipment

Battery ignition, starter, lights, including combination rear light and taillamp, vertically adjusted drawbar, non-upholstered hydraulic seat, muffler, 14.00x30 rear tires, and 6.50x18 front tires

Attachments and Special Features

TA, power steering, independent or transmission-type PTO, swinging drawbar, deluxe foam rubber seat, Hydra Touch, remote control (one, two, or three valves), air pipe extension, belt pulley, collector precleaner, spark arrester, radiator shutter, wheel weights, service meter, Electrall, fuel-gauge filler cap, and a variety of tire equipment

Major Changes/Dates

Information not available

Comments

None

International W-450 Diesel

Engine	D-281
Cylinders	four
Bore and stroke	4x5 1/4 inches
Displacement	281 cubic inches
Rated rpm	900–1,450
Compression ratio	16.5:1
Ignition	12-volt battery
Carburetor	IH diesel-starting
Cooling capacity	7 gallons
Fuel tank capacity	18 gallons
Horsepower ratings	na
Length	130 inches
Wheelbase	82 inches
Height	91 3/4 inches (at top of muffler)
Width	75 3/4 inches
Available treads	50 3/4 inches (front), 60 1/4 inches (rear)
Weight	6,000 pounds (no fuel or water)

Speed

Gear	Speed	
	regular	with TA
1	2.4 mph	1.6 mph
2	3.7 mph	2.5 mph
3	4.7 mph	3.1 mph
4	6.5 mph	4.4 mph

| 5 | 16.1 mph | 10.9 mph |
| Reverse | 3.2 mph | 2.2 mph |

Price	na
Nebraska test number	na
Numbers produced	1,108
Serial numbers	see IH W-450 listing
Chassis prefixes	W-450
Engine prefixes	D-281
Chassis serial number location	plate on left side of clutch housing
Engine serial number location	na

Regular Equipment
Battery ignition, starter, lights, including combination rear light and taillamp, vertically adjusted drawbar, non-upholstered hydraulic seat, muffler, 14.00x30 inch rear tires, and 6.50x18 front tires

Attachments and Special Features
TA, power steering, independent or transmission-type PTO, swinging drawbar, deluxe foam rubber seat, Hydra Touch, remote control (one, two, or three valves), air pipe extension, belt pulley, collector precleaner, spark arrester, radiator shutter, wheel weights, service meter, Electrall, fuel-gauge filler cap, variety of tire equipment, steel wheels, safety light, drawbar extension plate, tachometer, and exhaust extension

Major Changes/Dates
Information not available

Comments
None

International 600

Engine	C-350
Cylinders	four
Bore and stroke	4 1/2x6 1/2 inches
Displacement	350 cubic inches
Rated rpm	1,500
Compression ratio	6.1:1
Ignition	12-volt battery
Carburetor	IH E-12
Cooling capacity	8 gallons
Fuel tank capacity	36 gallons
Horsepower ratings	na
Length	135 inches
Wheelbase	83 inches
Height	73 inches (at top of muffler)
Width	76 inches
Available treads	52 inches (front), 60 inches (rear)

INTERNATIONAL 600
The International 600 followed in the tradition of the Super WD-9 tractors, intended for the largest farms. These tractors are not very common today, due to the short production run and specialized market. State Historical Society of Wisconsin

Weight	6,170 pounds (shipping weight)
Speed	
Gear	*Speed*
1	2.4 mph
2	3.2 mph
3	4.5 mph
4	5.5 mph
5	15.8 mph
Reverse	2.9 mph
Price	na
Nebraska test number	na
Numbers produced	
1956	1,484
1957	32
Serial numbers	
1956	501–1985
Chassis prefixes	600
Engine prefixes	C-350
Chassis serial number location	plate on right side of fuel tank and air cleaner support
Engine serial number location	right side of crankcase above ignition unit

Regular Equipment

Diesel, gasoline, distillate, or kerosene engine; disc-type differential foot brakes; battery ignition; starter; lights; muffler; fenders; vertically adjustable drawbar; jute-upholstered hydraulic- and spring-cushioned seat; weather cap; 14.00x34 rear tires; and 7.50x18 front tires

Attachments and Special Features

Transmission-driven PTO, power steering, one- or two-valve Hydra Touch, deluxe foam rubber seat, cigar lighter, air pipe extension, belt pulley, hand-operated over-center clutch, foot-operated decelerator, collector pre-cleaner, exhaust extension, magneto ignition, high-altitude pistons, pre-screener, radiator shutter, tachometer and hour meter, spark arrester, wheel weights, extension tires for rear steel wheels, spade lugs for rear wheels, scrapers for rear steel wheels, heavy-duty rear axles, swinging drawbar, safety light, break-away electrical connector, large-capacity tool box, seat springs, and low-boiling-point thermostat and heat indicator

Major Changes/Dates

Information not available

Comments

None

International 600 Diesel

Engine	D-350
Cylinders	four
Bore and stroke	4 1/2x5 1/2 inches
Displacement	350 cubic inches
Rated rpm	1,500
Compression ratio	15.6:1
Ignition	12-volt battery
Carburetor	IH diesel starting carburetor
Cooling capacity	9 gallons
Fuel tank capacity	35 gallons
Horsepower ratings	na
Length	135 inches
Wheelbase	83 inches
Height	88 inches
Width	76 inches
Available treads	52 inches (front), 60 inches (rear)
Weight	6,500 pounds (shipping weight)

Speed

Gear	Speed
1	2.4 mph
2	3.2 mph

3 ....4.5 mph
4 ....5.5 mph
5 ....15.8 mph
Reverse ....2.9 mph
Price ....na
Nebraska test number...................................na
Numbers produced.......................................na
Serial numbers ....see IH 600 listing
Chassis prefixes 600-D
Engine prefixes...D-350
Chassis serial number location ....right side of fuel tank support
Engine serial number location......................left side of engine above injection pump

Regular Equipment

Diesel, gasoline, distillate, or kerosene engine; disc-type differential foot brakes; battery ignition; starter; lights; muffler; fenders; vertically adjustable drawbar; jute-upholstered hydraulic- and spring-cushioned seat; weather cap; 14.00x34 rear tires; and 7.50x18 front tires

Attachments and Special Features

Transmission-driven PTO, power steering, one- or two-valve Hydra Touch, deluxe foam rubber seat, cigar lighter, air pipe extension, belt pulley, hand-operated over-center clutch, foot-operated decelerator, collector pre-cleaner, exhaust extension, magneto ignition, pre-screener, radiator shutter, tachometer and hour meter, spark arrester, wheel weights, extension tires for rear steel wheels, spade lugs for rear wheels, scrapers for rear steel wheels, heavy-duty rear axles, swinging drawbar, fuel-gauge filler cap, safety light, break-away electrical connector, different seat springs, and large-capacity tool box

Major Changes/Dates

Information not available

Comments

None

International 650

Engine...C-350 vertical inline
Cylinders ....four
Bore and stroke..4 1/2x5 1/2 inches
Displacement ....350 cubic inches
Rated rpm 1,500
Compression ratio...6.12
Ignition..12-volt battery and distributor
Carburetor..1 3/8-inch IH
Cooling capacity ....8 gallons

Fuel tank capacity ....36 gallons
Horsepower ratings
    Drawbar ....57.87 (Nebraska corrected maximum)
    PTO/belt ....65.17 (Nebraska corrected maximum)
Length...135 inches
Wheelbase...83.5 inches
Height ....88 inches (at top of muffler)
Width ....76 inches
Available treads ....52 inches (front), 60 inches(rear)
Weight ....6,170 pounds
Speed

Gear	Speed
1	2.4 mph
2	3.2 mph
3	4.5 mph
4	5.5 mph
5	15.8 mph
Reverse	2.9 mph

Price ....na
Nebraska test number.....................................618
Numbers produced
    1956 and 1957 2,561
    1958...2,372
Serial numbers
    1956...501–687
    1957...688–3451 or 688–3470
    1958...3471–5433
Chassis prefixes 650
Engine prefixes...C-350
Chassis serial number location ....right side of fuel tank support
Engine serial number location.......................right side of engine above ignition unit

Regular Equipment

Diesel, gasoline, distillate, or kerosene engine; disc-type differential foot brakes; battery ignition; starter; lights; muffler; fenders; vertically adjustable drawbar; jute-upholstered hydraulic- and spring-cushioned seat; weather cap; 14.00x34 rear tires; and 7.50x18 front tires

Attachments and Special Features

Transmission-driven PTO, power steering, one- or two-valve Hydra Touch, deluxe foam rubber seat, cigar lighter, air pipe extension, belt pulley, hand-operated over-center clutch, foot-operated decelerator, collector pre-cleaner, exhaust extension, magneto ignition, high-altitude pistons, pre-screener, radiator shutter, tachometer and hour meter, spark arrester, wheel weights, extension tires for rear steel wheels, spade lugs and extensions for rear steel wheels, scrapers for rear steel wheels, heavy-duty rear axle, swinging drawbar, variety of wheel and tire equipment, front and rear steel wheels, large-capacity tool box, safety light, break-away electrical connector, detachable seat pad, and deluxe detachable seat pad

Major Changes/Dates
First gas 650 was probably number 1044
Last straight 650 was probably number 5040; the rest were diesel or LPG

Comments
None

International 650 Diesel

Engine	D-350
Cylinders	four
Bore and stroke	4 1/2x5 1/2 inches
Displacement	350 cubic inches
Rated rpm	1,500
Compression ratio	15.6:1
Ignition	12-volt battery
Carburetor	IH diesel starting carburetor
Cooling capacity	9 gallons
Fuel tank capacity	35 gallons
Horsepower ratings	na
Length	135 inches
Wheelbase	83 inches
Height	88 inches (at top of muffler)
Width	76 inches
Available treads	52 inches (front), 60 inches (rear)
Weight	6,500 pounds (shipping weight)

Speed

Gear	Speed
1	2.4 mph
2	3.2 mph
3	4.5 mph
4	5.5 mph
5	15.8 mph
Reverse	2.9 mph

Price	na
Nebraska test number	na
Numbers produced	na
Serial numbers	see IH 650 listing
Chassis prefixes	650-D
Engine prefixes	D-350
Chassis serial number location	right side of fuel tank support
Engine serial number location	left side of engine above injection pump

Regular Equipment

Diesel, gasoline, distillate, or kerosene engine; disc-type differential foot brakes; battery ignition; starter; lights; muffler; fenders; vertically adjustable drawbar; jute-upholstered hydraulic- and spring-cushioned seat; weather cap; 14.00x34 rear tires; and 7.50x18 front tires

Attachments and Special Features

Transmission-driven PTO, power steering, one- or two-valve Hydra Touch, deluxe foam rubber seat, detachable seat pad, deluxe detachable seat pad, seat springs, cigar lighter, air pipe extension, belt pulley, hand-operated over-center clutch, foot-operated decelerator, collector pre-cleaner, exhaust extension, magneto ignition, pre-screener, radiator shutter, tachometer and hour meter, spark arrester, wheel weights, extension tires for rear steel wheels, spade lugs, scrapers for rear steel wheels, heavy-duty rear axle, swinging drawbar, variety of wheel and tire equipment, front and rear steel wheels, watch-dog fuel filter, safety light, and break-away electrical connector

Major Changes/Dates

Information not available

Comments

None

International 650 LPG

Engine	C-350
Cylinders	four
Bore and stroke	4.4x5 1/2 inches
Displacement	350 cubic inches
Rated rpm	1,500
Compression ratio	8.25:1
Ignition	12-volt battery
Carburetor	IH 1-3/8-inch
Cooling capacity	9 gallons
Fuel tank capacity	42 gallons
Horsepower ratings	
Drawbar	60.71 (Nebraska corrected maximum)
PTO/belt	67.02 (Nebraska corrected maximum)
Length	135 inches
Wheelbase	83 inches
Height	88 inches (at top of muffler)
Width	76 inches
Available treads	52 inches (front), 60 inches (rear)
Weight	6,700 pounds (shipping weight)

Speed

Gear	Speed
1	2.4 mph
2	3.2 mph
3	4.5 mph
4	5.5 mph
5	15.8 mph
Reverse	2.9 mph

Price ....na
Nebraska test number...................................621
Numbers produced.......................................na
Serial numbers ....see IH 650 listing
Chassis prefixes 650-L
Engine prefixes...C-350
Chassis serial number location ....plate on right side of fuel tank and air cleaner support
Engine serial number location.......................right side of crankcase above ignition unit

Regular Equipment

Disc-type differential foot brakes, battery ignition, starter, lights, muffler, fenders, vertically adjustable drawbar, jute-upholstered hydraulic- and spring-cushioned seat, weather cap, 14.00x34 rear tires, and 7.50x18 front tires

Attachments and Special Features

Transmission-driven PTO, power steering, one- or two-valve Hydra Touch, deluxe foam rubber seat, cigar lighter, air pipe extension, belt pulley, hand-operated over-center clutch, foot-operated decelerator, collector pre-cleaner, exhaust extension, magneto ignition, high-altitude pistons, pre-screener, radiator shutter, tachometer and hour meter, spark arrester, wheel weights, extension tires for rear steel wheels, spade lugs and extensions for rear steel wheels, scrapers for rear steel wheels, heavy-duty rear axle, swinging drawbar, variety of wheel and tire equipment, and front and rear steel wheels

Major Changes/Dates

First LPG tractor was probably number 1275

Comments

None

Appendix

Recommended Books

Fay, Guy. *International Harvester Experimental and Prototype Tractors.*
Motorbooks International, 1996
Gay, Larry. *Farm Tractors 1975–1995.* American Society of Agricultural
Engineers, 1995
Gray, R. B. *The Agricultural Tractor: 1855-1950.* U.S. Department of Agri-
culture, 1954
Larsen, Lester. *Farm Tractors 1950–1975.* American Society of Agricultural
Engineers, 1981
Marsh, Barbara. *A Corporate Tragedy,* originally published by Doubleday
& Company, 1985; reprint available from Binder Books (503/684-2024)
Wendel, C. H. *150 Years of International Harvester.* Crestline, 1981

Clubs

IH Collectors (also publishes *Harvester Highlights*)
Membership Department
310 Busse Hwy., Suite 250
Park Ridge, IL 60068-3251
847/823-8612 (evenings)
847/683-0207 (FAX)

Magazines

Red Power
Box 277
Battle Creek, IA 51006

Antique Power
P.O. Box 1000
Westerville, OH 43081-7000
614/848-5038

Belt Pulley
P.O. Box 83
Nokomis, IL 62075
217/563-2612

Engineers and Engines
2240 Oak Leaf St.
P.O. Box 2757
Joliet, IL 60434-2757

Gas Engine
P.O. Box 328
Lancaster, PA 17608
717/392-0733

Successful Farming
1716 Locust Street
LS416
Des Moines, IA 50309
800/374-3276

*For a complete listing of tractor models,
see table of contents*